Builders
of Our Land

A Movement
to Restore America's
Land of Opportunity

Lee V. Byberg

For Nancy, Kristoffer, Anders, Steffen, and Shauna
For All Friends of the American Dream

Contents

Acknowledgments

I am grateful for the love and support of many people on this journey. I am most grateful to Nancy, my wife and best friend, who has always supported me in the pursuit of my dreams. I am hopeful that our three boys and their generation will see me standing FOR THEM. Thanks to my parents for living out humility, the path to wisdom and faith in Christ. I am also grateful for the Nybergs (in-laws) for always being near when needed.

What I have become, and what I am, would have been much less without my mentors, Ted Huisinga and Ray Norling. Neither could I have taken a pause from my professional career to forge this movement to restore America's land of opportunity without the friendships from my "partners" Rick Huisinga, Scott Norling, and Torry Norling.

Pastor Keith Kerstetter and Pastor Bruce Schoeman mean more to me than they will ever imagine. Thanks to Bob Poe and the other leaders from Decision Makers for believing and praying that America can be restored.

Thanks to the advisory and accountability board (Nancy Haapoja, John Chapin, Pastor Tony Freeburg, and Paul Aasness) for going deep and being committed well beyond normal expectations. I have fond memories of my first campaign team from 2010. It was a fun ride. Much appreciation to the 2012 team for daring to think differently.

And finally, to the many leaders from all walks of life who told their stories to enrich our America, I thank you!

Introduction

News headlines scream every day that we are a world in crisis. The United States faces severe economic, social, and political stress as never before in our history.

We are losing more of our income through higher taxes and slower economic growth.

Restrictive regulations are choking the life out of our businesses.

Productivity is being penalized.

Our debt is growing.

China is taking over.

But in the midst of so much going wrong, I believe we are also at a time of great opportunity. We can create the America we want. It will take true vision and leadership. I have the vision, which I will share in this book. The vision is for America to return to her moral roots, relying on the independent character of her people to excel. We are going in the opposite direction in many respects, and I believe we must make drastic changes now. If we do not, we will find ourselves in a position our forefathers never dreamed.

It will require leadership to help us realize this vision and reclaim America. After all, true leadership is the ability to guide others to a destination they would not go on their own. I know for certain, with the direction this country is going in today, that we will not head to a place of prosperity, principle, and purpose on our own. I am ready to be a guide to help us go in a different direction than we are headed.

But I am not the only one who knows we are going in the wrong direction. Individuals all over this country realize the state America is in and they see the decline as it is happening, but many communities seem unable to change course because of those who lead. America is crying for real change. Not just change for change's sake. But change back to what she once was.

I believe that the original American values and ideals are best embodied by my neighbors in the heartland. Those original values that make America unique in the world took root in the heartland and never let go. And that is why my purpose is to restore our nation by leading a movement from within Minnesota's heartland.

This movement to reclaim America will look to the heartland to remind us what we used to have, where we went wrong, and what we need to do to regain that which made us great. This American movement will help us restore faith, family, and free enterprise.

Many of us may get involved in this movement because of fear — fear that our great country is crumbling, fear that our way of life will be lost, fear that we no longer will be exceptional. That fear can drive us to act. But when our struggle becomes grueling or the costs start to mount, as often happens in times of great change, that fear will not be enough to sustain us. It is then that the other strong human force, love, must show up. We may start this movement because of fear, but we endure and persevere because of love. Love is the single most important and single most capable force to carry us through the days ahead. It is our love of God, family, and this country that will give us the strength, courage, and the will to stand.

It is imperative for this movement to sweep this country. The need is clear and the time is now. America is racing toward financial and moral bankruptcy, and some would argue that we may already be there. I don't believe we are there yet, but we are too close to those certain futures if we do not act now.

We cannot afford to wait any longer and we cannot simply stand by and accept defeat. This movement arises from the keen sense of awareness we have in the heartland, knowing what is at stake.

We must not rest until we restore America.

Our movement to restore America cannot happen with only me or only you. It will take all of us. It will require our best — our time, our money, and our influence. The only way we can fulfill the challenge of altering the very course of this country's history is to use everything we have to make changes in policy, in budgeting, and in American culture. It's not enough to sit around our kitchen tables and remember the good, old days. We must remind America of those days and return her to them.

It is time that we bring America to D.C.

Come join me.

CHAPTER 1
America's Game

It's fitting that this book starts and ends with an analogy using America's favorite pastime, baseball. We have two teams facing off, America's We the People Team against the star closer from the Centralized Federal Government Team. The star closer is President Barack Obama. He is ready to transform and finish the game. It is the bottom of the ninth inning. The Centralized Federal Government Team is leading 3-0. The bases are loaded. Can the People's Team come back? The count is 2 outs. One more out and it is over.

America's team has limited government on first base. It is a long way to home plate. A long time has passed since we had a limited federal government for the people. The player on first base can hardly remember how free and strong they used to be when they were allowed to make decisions on their own.

On second base, free enterprise is representing America's Team. The second base player looks a bit better than the first base player. Free enterprise is comprised of small business owners and the entrepreneurs who take risks and create most of the jobs in our nation. But free enterprise is also comprised of medium-to-large companies. Many of the larger companies have by now accepted big government and the expensive regulations. They actually have learned to take advantage of the expensive regulations and use them against the smaller companies who cannot carry the burden. Many of the big companies actually give just as much in donations to big government political candidates as small government candidates. Nevertheless, free enterprise as a player still remembers the feeling of being free to explore, take chances, fail, succeed, and grow. The free enterprise player is hoping for a grand slam to bring them all home.

On third base, we have America's families. These are the people who work day by day to make a living. Many of them have forgotten how they used to be free and self-sufficient. They are not sure how hard they want to play against the star closer. After all, why worry when the star closer and the Central Government team promised them that all will be fine regardless of the outcome of the game. But when you look a

16

little closer, behind some of the confusion, behind some of the struggling families, there is still fire in the eyes of many people. They are ready to run all the way home. They not only remember freedom and opportunity. They not only hope for a grand slam. They are praying for a grand slam. You can see them seek a Higher Power, as they pray in humility, as they reach out to each other. "God bless our America. We will get back on your side, God. Lord, give us speed and strength to reach home plate. Forgive us for our negligence. Give us another chance, and we will restore our nation. We will bring you back into our families, our schools, and into our government."

The count remains two outs. President Obama needs only one more strike or a chase to end the game. He is the closer. Many star pitchers came before him to give him the lead. All he needs to do is to finish the game. All he needs to do is to transform the nation for good. No going back. As a closer, all he needs to do is to prevent the farmer from hitting the ball out of the park. If he can throw a strike or fool the farmer to chase a ball, he wins regardless.

Who wins the game for America's soul? I can't say yet. Much work remains before we can win our game. This is time to become primal about America. This is time to be in love with America. This is time to rebuild our land. I pray that the words contained in this book will lift your spirit and call you to action. I know that the historical American framework described herein will renew your mind. And I know that the stories of people overcoming obstacles to better themselves and their communities will surely inspire all of us to become better versions of ourselves.

CHAPTER 2

The American Experiment

The American Dream is a notion unlike any other in the world. It is so much a part of our culture that we never consider that it's not something others enjoy in their countries.

The American Dream is the notion that we can have happy and successful lives if we work hard. It came from the very fact that the founding document of our nation professed each and every person's right to life, liberty, and the pursuit of happiness. So stated the Declaration of Independence: "We hold these truths to be self-evident, that all men are created equal, that they are endowed by their Creator with certain unalienable rights, that among these are life, liberty, and the pursuit of happiness."

The American Dream was the basis of our nation's independence and the moral standard we established for ourselves and to which no other nation could stand. It was the draw that attracted millions to our shores over the centuries, as America stands unique in its promise.

It is an ideal so compelling that it is part of what makes us special. Many who do not see the specialness of our nation would wonder how it is that we alone can hold ourselves up as to embody the concept of opportunity for freedom and happiness. What about the German dream or the French dream or the Irish dream? They wonder.

Do those people not have dreams? Of course they have dreams. That is not the point. The point here is that no other nation approaches individual freedom quite the way we do. Other nations have various traditional, societal, and cultural restrictions on individuals that prevent citizens from attaining success far beyond their "station" in life or status would allow. A person born into a lower ranked family is not inclined to rise above that ranking, no matter how hard he works or how smart he becomes. That is unless such person is willing to break through the limitations of the societal station and its alluring promise of comfort.

It's different in America. Here, your pursuit of success isn't limited by the family you were born into or the actions of ancestors who came before you. People who were born into poverty have ascended to the highest positions in our government. Abraham Lincoln, our 16th president, was born into poverty in Kentucky. Where else in the world can this happen?

America is unique as a nation upholding personal liberty. This notion is called the American exceptionalism. We have been challenged, even by fellow Americans, to not uphold America as something grander, better than other nations. Such critics claim that this belief in exceptionalism is arrogant and demeaning to other nations. The truth, however, is the opposite. This is not about ranking or comparing America with other nations.

The American uniqueness is its discovery, proclamation, and willingness to risk it all for individual liberty. For the first time in history, humanity of past, current, and future generations could learn and/or come to a place that is the home of the free. America's exceptionalism is forged in the Declaration of Independence. The idea of the individual being lifted up in value second only to the Creator. This is humility. There was no room for the arrogance from government, from ruling classes, from the elite, from the bureaucrats, or from an earthly king. It was about "we the people." Our self-worth, dignity, and very being crafted as unalienable rights. This was America kneeling in humility to in God we trust.

No other nation holds the promise — and fulfillment of that promise — of life, liberty, and the pursuit of happiness. Many nations have structures that are built on dynasties or powerful families and access to certain positions, opportunities, and resources are limited, not by a person's willingness to work, but by factors beyond his control, including whether he is lucky enough to have been born into the right dynasty or powerful family.

But here in America, we believe that there are certain rights we all have that cannot be granted by government or society or tradition. Those rights have been granted by our Creator. We have those rights by virtue of being born. We believe in the dignity of the individual and the individual's right to pursue a good life. That is what makes America special.

And that is the basis of the American Dream.

Self-governance

Does this mean everyone will attain the American Dream? Of course not. There is no guarantee. But you are offered the freedom to pursue. Europe has this notion that the government will take care of you from cradle to death. And because of that, there is the mentality that government tells you what to do because it gives you so much.

We can't truly have the freedom to pursue happiness when we owe so much of our lives to government. That is the danger that awaits us here. We are slowly becoming more and more beholden to government, as government expands to encompass so much of our daily lives. To the uninformed, the expansion of government seems harmless. Many people wonder what is so wrong about government healthcare, expansive regulation, and entitlements. The problem with all those things is that the more government gives you, the less freedom you have. You may not initially feel that loss of freedom because your mind may be so clouded by all of what you think government has given you. But the moment you want to exercise your own freedom of choice and it goes against what government wants you to do, then you realize you have given up your freedom.

It's like an adult child living at home with his parents. Sure, he may think he is getting a great deal because his parents are paying for his housing, his meals, and everything else, but what happens when he doesn't do something his parents want him to do? What happens if he comes home later than they want or he dates someone they don't like or he skips a function they want him to attend? Well, they have it within their rights to put undue pressure on him to do what they want. Why? Because they take care of him.

And that is the danger of too much control. Self-governance is undermined when the federal government makes all the decisions or takes care of us. Self-governance on the individual level is the individual's ability to make decisions about personal conduct and life, without interference from government. Self-governance on the local level is the ability of local communities to make decisions about what is best for them without interference from the federal government. The opportunity for self-governance is very important to the pursuit of happiness and the American Dream. When government tries to barge in on our lives and tell us what to do, government is trying to take away our freedom of choice and our ability to make our own decisions. In such an instance, government, in essence, is trying to run our lives, take away our liberty, and limit the pursuit of happiness. Government is trying to go against the very spirit of this nation.

What do you think happens when the majority of the population is dependent on government? They will vote for politicians who will promise them even more programs and take away even more liberty. But there are strings attached. Government tells you it is there to fix your problems, but fixing your problems comes at a price.

I asked my 22-year-old son the other day, "How does it feel to be American and 22 years old?" He said, "Dad, it feels like we live in a big black box. We are blind, and we don't know it. I have friends who can work, but they would rather receive a check from the government and do nothing. And I have friends who are looking for work, but cannot find anyone to hire them."

Our youth are indeed facing a dire situation, with record high unemployment and student loan debt. These problems may contain much more than a short-term challenge as they have the potential to destroy the well-being and drive of a generation.

Let me point out to those who are looking for work and not finding. Opportunities for employment do exist in production agriculture. But it is work. For those who are willing to start or pursue a career in production agriculture, there are opportunities if you are willing to show up for work every day, if you are trustworthy, willing to accept responsibility, committed to on-the-job training programs, and if you thrive in challenging circumstances adjusting to never-ending changes from the elements in nature.

I believe the price of the "big black box" is too high to pay. It is destroying our American dream. We cannot let government take away our liberty or our pursuit of happiness. We must protect self-governance. Right now, we are in danger of becoming the generation that will lose freedom and will lose liberty.

CHAPTER 3

My Story

I was born in the United States but my family left when I was young. My parents were Christian missionaries to Brazil and Paraguay, so that's where I grew up. We eventually moved to my parents' native Norway, where my father was pastor of churches in the Telemark and Rogaland regions. So I had a childhood of diverse experiences, from playing with neighborhood children in Paraguay   learning local customs to getting to know relatives in Norway. I returned to the United States the year I turned 20 and attended the Carlson School of Management at the University of Minnesota. I received a Bachelor of Science and an MBA there.

I chose Minnesota in large part because I had family in Sunburg and Spicer. I returned to America by choice as a young man, and made my life here. In many ways, it was like I was an immigrant coming here, because life was so different from what I was accustomed to in other places. Like others coming to America from a foreign land, I left behind country, family, and culture.

All for the American Dream. But I never focused on what I was giving up, but welcomed what I was gaining. I was gaining the opportunity to live my life as a man free to create his own path and make his own way. I've lived in America 30 years, and she has given me all I could have asked for, and more.

Freedom to choose

College friends introduced me to the American idea that you can be anything you want to be if you work hard enough, develop skills based on your talents, and get along with others. It was a spirit different from anything I had experienced before in South America and Europe.

These friends came from very modest backgrounds, but they had this idea that they could do anything in life. Whatever they dreamt about was not limited by family background or class or economic means. I saw this in two of my best friends. One grew up on a dairy farm in South Dakota and one had a dad with a car dealership. I remember thinking, what gives them the guts to think they can do anything? But that is America in a nutshell.

I fell in love with the freedom that it is up to you. That there is nothing holding you back.

And so I set about to make my life. It didn't matter that I didn't come from a wealthy family or that I had spent my childhood overseas. It didn't matter that my parents had been more concerned with building treasure in heaven than amassing wealth on earth. It didn't even matter that I had to brush up on my English to become more proficient when I returned from overseas.

All that mattered was that I was willing to work hard, build relationships, and create value in the lives of others.

So I settled in Willmar with my wife. We became active in church life there and in our community. We raised our three boys, who all graduated from or are attending Willmar High School. We got to be a part of the American Dream.

I've worked in various corporate capacities in Willmar. I am vice president of operations at Life-Science Innovations, the parent company of Willmar Poultry Company. Before taking up that position, I experienced one of my largest professional accomplishments where, as general manager of Willmar Poultry Company, I oversaw the expansion of turkey egg production from 10 million a year to 25 million a year in Minnesota. This meant new jobs, more food for families, and a stronger investment in our communities.

In another instance, when negotiations broke down during the purchase of a Minnesota regional state hospital, I helped to restore communication that ultimately led to the purchase of that hospital and the creation of MinnWest Technology Campus.

I'll tell you more about that later in this book. But for now, know that our aim there was to create jobs for the next generation of workers in our local community. MinnWest Technology Campus is a cluster campus concept with an atmosphere of learning, innovation, and cooperation, as MinnWest brings together students, educators, companies, and others to collaborate and grow.

With more than 30 business tenants and more than 360 employees, the campus is fulfilling our dream of creating jobs — for now and the future.

But my commitment to America and the area didn't stop at my business endeavors.

I felt so strongly about my love for America that I became a songwriter!

In September 2009, I wrote 12 songs sharing my love for this country. Fifteen other people from the community stepped in and helped with the production of the CD over the next two months, even turning a room in my house into a temporary music studio. That experience was just another example of the American can-do spirit that I love.

I describe part of my story in the lyrics of my song titled, "Twice American." We can all be twice American, whether we are born American or become American.

We become twice American, first through our legal rights, and second, by living out the American spirit. I truly believe that we must now engage in a movement to restore America to her ideals to ensure future generations have the opportunity to become twice American.

We can't let their rights be trampled on or the spirit of freedom become only something they read about in history books.

My story, an American coming from foreign lands, makes me highly sensitive to just how special our country is. I have lived the difference. I know we are not just one country among all others in the world. We are the only country with the spirit we have.

I am very concerned that my three boys will not enjoy the opportunities and liberty that America has offered me. I want them to experience their versions of my story. I want them to be able to decide to be whatever they want and to actually have a shot at making that happen. But I am just as concerned for all the other children in this country, the next generation. We can't leave them an America that offers them fewer rights and opportunities than we had.

Freedom and opportunity have joined together to create my story.

I want the same for the next generation.

CHAPTER 4

Marriage

Nancy and I met for the first time in November of 1983 at Annie's Parlor Restaurant in Dinkytown, near the University of Minnesota. She was a student at North Central University in Minneapolis, pursuing a degree in Elementary and Early Childhood Education, while I was enrolled at the Carlson School of Management at the University of Minnesota. On that particular evening, we were both hanging out with friends at Annie's Parlor. I was sitting at a table with some male friends when a waitress approached us with some good news. The waitress explained that since the restaurant was full, she hoped we would be kind enough to offer a few girls the chance to dine with us in our booth.

We, of course, welcomed the opportunity to entertain those unfortunate gals whose luck just turned for the better. Nancy introduced herself as Nancy Nyberg, and I introduced myself, using my Norwegian name "Vidar" Byberg. Nancy told me later that she heard me introduce myself as "Myberg" and added my name by the "M" in her address book. That was the first day of Nancy lifelong project to soften my Norwegian-Minnesota accent. I just remind people I had to go to Norway to learn the original Minnesota accent!

After the entertaining evening at Annie's Parlor came to an end, we exchanged phone numbers. Little did Nancy know that her childhood prayer not to "give up" her family name was enroute to fulfillment. After all, changing only one letter from Nyberg to Byberg is a pretty close fulfillment. Our friendship started with going out to movies, attending church services, and studying together at the Wilson Library. I also helped her with research papers and she helped me with my English (as she still does).

During the summer of 1986, Nancy came back to Minnesota after a six-week mission trip working with children in Jamaica. I meet her this time at the Christian Music Festival (Sonshine) in Willmar. She had a nice tan, hair in a ponytail (which is the look I still love the most), blue eyes, and a big smile. She had on a white and yellow outfit and as usual, plenty of entertaining stories. I can still see her standing there in the sun together with her best girlfriend, Jan. That summer, I agreed to join her on a canoe trip with a group from her church youth group. We went canoeing into the beautiful Boundary Waters in Northern Minnesota.

The weather during the canoe trip was so-so, but the rain did not stop Nancy from her main mission in life: entertaining and taking care of others. She sat in the middle of our three-person canoe, as she preferred to do less of the paddling and more of the talking. Her friend Missy paddled from up front, while I managed the back end of the canoe. After a few days of working the waters throughout God's nature and listening to Nancy's stories, I asked her if it would be OK for us all to enjoy some quiet time of reflection as we navigated the remaining waters. Well, she accepted my request but was clearly upset that I could be so rude. She went silent for the rest of the day to prove her point! I can only recount one other day where Nancy felt like being quiet. I have since learned my lesson of not depriving her of the gift of sharing.

Eventually Nancy forgave my rudeness and resumed telling stories again the very next day on the canoe trip. One day after coming home from the Boundary Waters, I made up my mind. I asked Nancy for a conversation, took her hand, and proceeded with a serious monologue. My plan was not necessarily to turn this into a one-man speech, but that's how it turned out as Nancy mostly listened to me as I shared my heart's feelings and commitment. This day turned out to be Nancy's second quietest day in her life. She told me later that her hand was clammy during our talk, or more correctly, my chat. I was too preoccupied to notice the clammy hands, as I was expressing a bright future for both of us. I had made up my mind to pursue Nancy as my personal "story teller," friend, and companion. It was not a marriage proposal, but the beginning of our courtship. Yes, it was about wonderful feelings of romance and being in love. But it was about more than that. It was about proposing to change our relationship from "friends" status to boyfriend-girlfriend. It was dating with the intention of marriage.

After dating for two years, I proposed to Nancy at the Carousel restaurant in St. Paul. This time, she was not silent or reflecting. She answered yes without hesitation. The necessary ground work between us was already built through our courtship. For me, my proposal to Nancy involved another major decision. Yes it was about love, about commitment, but also about choosing where to live the rest of my life. This was also about choosing America. It was about being Twice American. I was first born American by chance (as none of us have the option to choose our birthplace). Having lived on two other continents, I knew I could live and do well pretty much wherever I wanted. At this time I became Twice American – and such by choice. I loved my story telling girl, loved the country which made her the way she is, and wanted to live in the freest county in the world. Nancy accepted my proposal.

Nancy and I married in Willmar on June 10, 1989. The wedding was held at her Methodist church in Willmar. We agreed that America would be our permanent home, but Nancy expressed an interest in living in Norway for a few years to learn part of my heritage, which is also her heritage.

Our first two boys, Kristoffer and Anders, were born in Minnesota. Of the five of us, only our son Steffen was born in Norway. Nancy could tell you stories about giving birth in Norway, about laughing gas used in the Norwegian hospitals, but she would need to write her own book. Steffen claims however to be the only true Viking in our family, and we don't disagree with him. While we lived in Norway during those three years, Nancy learned much about the culture and background which has influenced the Minnesota culture.

We raised four children in Willmar. Our own three sons are very different. I think God must have lots of humor and/or is amused by "stretching" us as parents while we attempt to figure out what works for one child versus another. I tell my boys, "I will treat you fair, but not the same because you are all different." What is good for one of you is not necessarily good for your brother(s). Kristoffer has my business drive, his grandpa Byberg's practical side and grandma Nyberg's servant attitude. Anders has my serious side and sense of fairness, his grandpa Nyberg's interest in facts and logic and his grandma Byberg's self-discipline.

Steffen has Nancy's outgoing personality and his grandpa Byberg's interest in history, philosophy, and cultures. He is gifted with languages and music.

We had the privilege of raising a girl from age of 13 to 18. Shauna lost her father on her 12th birthday in a drowning incident on Green Lake. She attended the same school our boys did in Willmar. We stepped in and offered our home for Shauna so that she could remain in the community where she grew up. The experience was good for the boys as they had to learn how to live with a big sister. These years were very difficult years for Nancy as Shauna struggled through the typical teenage ways into adulthood. I don't think we would have made it through those challenging years without a conviction that we were supposed to do this for Shauna, for God, and for the community.

•

Nancy is the best parent in our family and my best friend. She outdoes me in everything. I have this feeling that perhaps there is a small chance she may think I outdo her in something. And as she does, we are both home free.

CHAPTER 5

Making a Living

I had many jobs growing up. No doubt these jobs helped me to discover and develop my talents for business and economics. I started my first "company" as a young boy while living in Paraguay. I was barely 10 at the time when together with my younger brother we launched our first production company. We used "just in time" inventory methods in our assembly line. It was serious yet "lofty" business. Our enterprise was to produce and market kites for the boys in our local community. When we later moved to Norway, I talked my farmer uncle Olav into hiring me to help out with his operation. Other jobs throughout my high school years included working in a bakery, retail sales, and in maintenance. I also was a newspaper delivery boy, retirement home worker, gas station employee, and steel mill worker. I enjoyed in particular the challenge with the "working men" at the steel mill in Telemark. The working conditions were as you could image. It was hotter than the Minnesota summer and the work would turn any boy into a man. The pay was great. These early years working in different fields helped me to learn how to get along with all kinds of people.

I received three job offers after completing the MBA program at the University of Minnesota in 1990 and accepted the offer from Coopers & Lybrand Consulting in Minneapolis. As a CPA and consulting firm, Coopers & Lybrand was a wonderful place as a "boot camp" for smart and driven individuals. Coopers provided the opportunity to gain experience in the audit department, tax department and the group of business investigations. During my nearly three-year engagement with Coopers & Lybrand, I was given the opportunity to play around with economic models. I soon discovered that I had a special knack for the development of such complex economic models.

My next employer was Phillips Petroleum Company. Phillips hired me as a staff economist to develop and manage economic models needed to justify large capital projects and to determine the economic life of various oil/gas fields.

Much of my work with Phillips involved helping engineers to assess the economic value of the various projects under consideration. I developed a user-friendly economic tool for engineers. The goal was to replace the "dinosaur" of a mainframe economic system with this smaller, faster, stand-alone spreadsheet economic model to equip engineers to do their own initial economic screening of their new projects.

By now, Nancy and I had stayed three years in Norway and it was time to move home to America. While I worked on options to transfer with Phillips to Bartlesville, Oklahoma, Nancy was praying and working to find opportunities for me in her hometown of Willmar. I am not sure what Nancy promised God, but she told her dad, Lyle Nyberg, she would find something for me in Willmar even if I had to work for a fast food joint. During the process of moving home to Minnesota or to Oklahoma, we came to Willmar to visit Nancy's family one weekend. We went to church and ran into Ted Huisinga. Ted was and still is the CEO of Life-Science Innovations and affiliated companies, including Willmar Poultry Company. Ted invited us to his home for lunch after church and the rest is history. I remember telling Nancy that she would not believe what I found in Willmar as I toured Willmar Poultry Company and affiliated companies. This group of affiliated companies was a private enterprise owned by the Huisinga and Norling families. They had worked together for 60 years, had strong leadership, driven by innovation, and represented the strong productive segment of America. Nancy chuckled and was not surprised at all that I found this "gem" of free enterprise in her hometown.

I not only admired the quality of the people which comprised the affiliated companies, but believed they could create even more value to community, owners, and employees by adding the process of optimization to their already well-functioning businesses. Both senior leaders and the upcoming generation lived out their Christian faith and conservative principles. This faith element was something I found appealing in my decision to join the affiliated companies. I discussed with Rick Huisinga the aspect of living a life that could bring together the realms of work, family, church, and the community without compartmentalizing them. Living a life of integrity is possible when we are able to live out our values in a consistent manner in all segments of life. Your son should be able to see you as the same father whenever he runs into you at work or at home. The magnitude of how we live out our values, faith, and principles in daily life may vary from realm to realm, but the core values must be consistent if we want a life of integrity. Integrity, after all means to be true in all, complete in all circumstances.

Ted Huisinga offered me basically a job on the spot and has now been my mentor for the past 18 years. Ted is famous for hiring for talent even when there may not be a particular job opening. His thinking is that talented people will through nature and dedication create their own jobs. The decision to leave Phillips to join a relatively small company was not easy. I truly enjoyed the almost "unlimited" scope and size in projects and opportunities offered by Phillips. A mentor I had with a Phillips leader helped to clear the path. He said, "I do see that this opportunity in Willmar could be good for you and your family. Why don't you go and let me know within two years if you want to come back to Phillips."

I learned from this leader that we should always allow and encourage people to do what is best for them. Employees will exceed your expectations and add maximum value to your company when they see you as a leader that is always looking out for what is best for them. You may have to "give up" some good people if you encourage them to "go free" when unique opportunities arise, but you will also be able to recruit, develop, and keep more extraordinary people when they know you are in their corner.

I started with Willmar Poultry Company as a financial-economic analyst. My first project involved creating an optimization model for the turkey processing plant. The goal was to create a model that on a daily basis would predict the "best plan" for the day. The model would consider the market values of whole birds and the various parts on a given day, the age, gender, weight distribution of the incoming flocks, the potential line speeds tied to various products, and the availability and composite of the labor force. After six months of almost full-time programming and testing, we were finally ready to launch the model to real life; ironically, we sold the processing plant soon thereafter.

We worked on several fronts to increase the strength of our company and turkey industry. Those efforts, which started as research to improve the quality of our turkey poults, later led to improving the world for other animal species. A new company was spun off to develop further our discoveries to all animal species. The Salmonella Newport Bacterial Extract became the first federally licensed vaccine in November of 2004. The new company has by now created about 60 technical, sales, research and management jobs to develop this platform technology. Its mission is to discover and develop original veterinary vaccines to improve animal health and food safety in an environment that values scientific creativity.

We've faced challenges at Willmar Poultry, and have had to overcome them. Our major customer — who accounted for 75% of our sales — changed ownership and dropped us as a supplier. We turned that challenge into an opportunity. We expanded sales into new regions to service household name customers nationwide. In a few years, we grew our production of turkey eggs on company farms in Minnesota from 10 million eggs to 25 million eggs.

The rapid growth was challenging and motivating. When a large order comes, you have to choose to accept it or to let it go. If you accept rapid growth, it takes a strong team to bring forth the expansion without reducing the quality or increasing the cost of the current business. We probably never would have expanded as we did but for losing our major customer. The magic of free enterprise is that you can turn potential disaster into tremendous opportunity.

The human spirit and intellect are wired to perform best under pressure. It is not by accident we say: "When it gets tough, that's when the tough gets going." Imminent danger or change is not something people seek by choice, but nevertheless often provides blessings in disguise. You will never know the golden gems awaiting you unless you pursue them.

These hidden gems are not revealed until after you experience the blessings of competition and the danger of change. Abrupt changes have the power to reshape your world to a better place. Take courage and free yourself from fear as you embrace such opportunities.

CHAPTER 6

Nation of Faith, Family, and Free Enterprise

An objective look at where America is today must begin with where America has been. We must start with how we came to be and then how we ended up in this place.

The basis of who we are is a nation of faith. In fact, we are about faith, family, and free enterprise. It's what the Founders worked so hard to give us.

Nation of faith

Many, as President Barack Obama has done, would claim that we are not a Christian nation. However, a simple review of our history will show that we always have been a nation built on Judeo-Christian principles, from the very beginning. The Founding Fathers made reference to this as a matter of fact on multiple occasions.

General George Washington, who would later become our first president, wrote on July 9, 1776 that colonels and commanding officers were to get chaplains so soldiers would pay attention to the teachings and even attend religious services. He said that he hoped every soldier would live in a way that was becoming of a Christian who was defending the rights of his country.[1]

Washington made it clear Christian faith should influence the actions of those under his command. This is an indication that Washington believed his acts of leadership and the actions of those who were fighting in our nation's quest for freedom, were to be governed by Judeo-Christian principles.

These principles are what actually gave our Founding Fathers the courage and strength to risk everything in the revolution. They had a Judeo-Christian view of right and wrong, and when they felt wronged, they rebelled against that wrong-doing. They had a view that the Creator was the

---

[1] George Washington, The Writings of George Washington, John C. Fitzpatrick, editor. (Washington: Government Printing Office, 1932) Vol. 5, p. 245, July 9, 1776 order.

ultimate rights giver and when the king abused his power, that gave them the justification to say that we choose to rebel because what is happening goes against our beliefs.

Founding Father John Adams wrote to Thomas Jefferson on June 28, 1813: "The general principles on which the fathers achieved independence, were the only principles in which that beautiful assembly of young men could unite, and these principles only could be intended by them in their address, or by me in my answer. And what were these general principles? I answer, the general principles of Christianity, in which all those sects were united, and the general principles of English and American liberty, in which all those young men united, and which had united all parties in America, in majorities sufficient to assert and maintain her independence."[2]

Adams shared this opinion well into the life of the young country. He had been deeply involved in the fight for liberty and establishing the new government. In fact, by the time he wrote this letter, the Constitution had been in place more than 20 years, and he had served as president more than a decade before that writing to Jefferson. So he spoke with authority and with the clarity of thought of viewing the Constitution in action.

It's not so much that we were founded to adhere to one religion or denominational thought, as the early colonists came to these shores to escape that type of governmental interference and control. Early settlers risked life and braved stormy seas to get away from government-controlled religion in the form of the Church of England. So we were not formed to force people to live according to one religion that the government chose. Instead, our country was founded based on Judeo-Christian principles. This is important to note because the very basis of our nation rests on this understanding. In fact, the government that was formed based on those Judeo-Christian principles ensures liberty for all, no

---

[2] John Adams, The Works of John Adams, Second President of the United States, Charles Francis Adams, editor (Boston: Little, Brown and Company, 1856), Vol. X, to Thomas Jefferson, June 28, 1813.

matter their spiritual leanings. That includes atheists, agnostics, and people of other religions and leanings. It's only because we were founded on Judeo-Christian principles that we can protect the religious liberty of all. America became the freest country of all. Once we understand this, we realize that to go away from those Judeo-Christian principles is to go away from our very history.

Well more than a century after this nation was formed, Supreme Court Justice David Brewer affirmed the United States to be a Christian nation when ruling in an employment dispute outlined in Church of the Holy Trinity v United States: "These, and many other matters which might be noticed, add a volume of unofficial declarations to the mass of organic utterances that this is a Christian nation."[3]

Our Constitution was written only for moral and religious people. It didn't command us with 10,000 regulations. It had a premise, a framework of life, liberty, and the pursuit of happiness.

Family is the basic foundation of our society

Our Founding Fathers, in their efforts to set up a loose federal government that did not overreach, sought to create a society where the individual was respected and the family could grow. They recognized that the family is the basic structure. Without family, we cannot grow, prosper, or develop into better individuals, communities, or country. Our families are where we first learn values and our families are the places where we first become acquainted with rules, structure, and acceptable behavior.

When families are weakened or torn apart, that has a direct impact on our local communities, states, and even our

---

[3] Holy Trinity Church v United States, 143 U.S. 457, 1892.

nation. Family is where traditions are passed down and it is where we gain cultural understanding. All of these are important to a strong society.

Our families are under threat in America right now. Increasing pressure to ignore faith, governmental entitlement programs that seek to control families, and regulations that seek to regulate free enterprise and in turn limit families' abilities to earn are all factors that face us today.

Free enterprise is the cornerstone of prosperity

So we have long been a nation based on Judeo-Christian principles, and who we are is deeply rooted in our faith. Family is the basic structure of our society. But we are not just a nation of faith and family; we are a nation of free enterprise. Free enterprise is important because it is the system on which our economic prosperity is built. When our free enterprise takes a hit, our prosperity takes a hit. And when our prosperity is threatened, our families suffer. We are now operating in a political climate that seeks to dramatically limit and hamper free enterprise.

The Founding Fathers were very clear when they drafted our Constitution. They gave the federal government very limited powers, which did not include clamping down on private business. Government is there to protect the rights of the individuals to engage in free enterprise and prosper; it should not be there to stand in the way of that prosperity. Many point to the economic crisis we've been in over the past few years as a reason to reduce free enterprise through more government control and regulation. But that collapse did not happen because of a lack of regulations. Regulations were in place and the problems still arose. Problems arose because of governmental changes that created a climate that allowed the abuses that led to an economic crisis.

Why should we believe that the federal government is in a better position to make decisions for us when it has shown a total inability to even balance its own books? And there is no evidence that the federal government makes better decisions than we do.

When you talk about the original framework of a small federal government based on the original premise of life, liberty, and the pursuit of happiness, the reaction in the media is that this is old-style thinking and that it is too simplistic. But I challenge that notion and say the opposite. The original American Constitution is the most sophisticated document ever seen in history because it is based on the premise that you, the individual, have qualities that allow you to be self-governed without someone else making decisions for you.

The document protects our rights to free enterprise. It allows each individual, township, and state to determine what is best for itself, rather than delegating those choices to the federal government.

When it comes to free enterprise, that is very important because it means individuals and local communities should decide about their businesses and commerce. How can a government regulator in Washington, D.C. know better than a western Minnesota farming community what is best for that community?

Life is connected through a moral code and without a moral code, we can't be self- governed. This is key to limited government. We cannot have liberty unless we have a moral code. That is yet another reason why the Founders built this country on the Judeo-Christian principles. These principles and faith were so much a part of the very fiber of the new nation they were building. But what of the last thing, the pursuit of happiness? Free enterprise gives us the avenues to pursue happiness. A moral code, limited government, and free enterprise all combine to create the character of our nation.

That's why this has to be a movement that is beyond politics. We must have people to say we will go back to these principles. We will get back to faith. We need to get back to family.

We need to get back to free enterprise. Without any of

that, without any of those three elements, we cannot be the America our Founders envisioned.

And that is where we are today.

Our faith, our families, and our free enterprise are all in jeopardy.

CHAPTER 7

The Answer to Big Government Is Local Solutions

Each time we add a governmental agency we increase inefficiency and add cost. We grow government and increase the need for new revenue, without a way to pay for the new agency, except with new taxation, in most instances.

We've seen massive growth in government at the agency level. We have 15 cabinet-level federal government agencies — six created by Republican presidents, seven created by Democratic presidents, and two created by George Washington, our first president. Presidents of both parties created these agencies, so this isn't about one party growing the government. Both parties are responsible. That's why the movement I describe isn't a movement of political parties. It is a movement of people. It's time that truly concerned Republicans, Democrats, and Independents come together to save our nation. The large — and growing — federal government is not sustainable.

Both partisan and bipartisan policies have contributed to our fiscal crisis. The only way for America to regain prosperity and freedom is if the American people force both parties to realign themselves to the original American principles of limited federal government and free enterprise. The Democratic Party with President Obama and the rest of the progressives has a long time ago left the principles which made America great. The Republican Party also contributed to our fiscal crisis through influence of "big government" proponents in the party.

Real solutions should therefore be celebrated regardless of who is the originator as long as the policies are crafted in the spirit of the American free market and limited government principles. Within this framework, we can seek and find bipartisanship because we are aligning ourselves with what it means to be Americans. The issue should never be that we have too many rich or middle to upper income people, but that we don't have enough people doing well and advancing in our economy.

Current trends heap new taxes on us and destroy self-reliance

Any attempts to increase tax rates and the overall cost to the economy are harmful to our nation and will reduce disposable income, reduce consumption, reduce GDP and reduce overall tax revenue. Presidents Ronald Reagan and George H.W. Bush demonstrated solid leadership. This was expected of them as champions of conservative principles and they allowed free enterprise to grow the economy and increase the overall tax revenue. Presidents John F. Kennedy and Bill Clinton showed brave leadership as they went against the "normal" flow of the Democratic Party and championed tax reductions. President Obama, however, has continued to demonstrate lack of understanding in economic principles and seems more concerned about winning the economic "class struggle." Obama's vision will make all worse off (both rich and poor) and demonstrate poor leadership contrasted with Kennedy who took the high road and did the best for the American economy even if meant going against the tax ideology of his party.

Our government is taking over lives in a way the founders never could have even envisioned. Or maybe they envisioned it and wrote a Constitution to prevent it. The Founders did not want a strong centralized government to take over the lives of its citizens. But as the years have rolled one into another, administrations have seen fit to add more and more government. One example of the increase in government is our current president's signing of the most massive healthcare legislation in our nation's history, legislation that guarantees government will remove any shred of self-governance from its people. This healthcare change, while touted as reform, is actually far from reform. It is moving further in the direction we've been going in, of more government taking us further and further away from our roots.

Several states challenged the constitutionality of the healthcare law, because those leaders realized it goes against not only the spirit of this nation but the letter of the law as outlined by our Founders. The law has been upheld as constitutional, but that does not mean the issue is dead. It means we must fight even harder to let reason prevail by repealing this legislation. But more on that later.

For now, I'll just say that the healthcare legislation flies in the face of whatever we know of the concept of limited government. Limited government is the only principle articulated in our Constitution that ensures the liberty promised in our Declaration of Independence. For if we have a centralized government that controls every aspect of our lives, then of course liberty is not possible. We no longer have the freedom to pursue the lives or happiness we want, when government grows too large or is too far-reaching, as in the case of the new healthcare law.

The growing of the federal government has been happening for many, many years but it doesn't have to continue.

Many would argue that the federal government has to have its hand in so many aspects of our lives because no other entity or structure can serve the needs of the people in this way.

It might be easy to believe that to be true, if we didn't have an example of a model that did not rely on governmental intrusion. We do have a model. It is America before such large social programs. America used to allow local communities to handle many of the things the federal government does today.

Local solutions are the answer to large government

I believe we can look to local organizations and learn from them. One such organization is Love INC. It's an example of what a community can do locally, between churches, between business leaders, and between organizations who decide together to bring solutions.

Churches and other faith-based organizations are an integral part of any local community, and I believe the community of faith will play an important part in restoring America. One specific way this can happen is when faith-based organizations become part of the healing of our local communities. This used to be the standard, from the founding of our country up until too much government regulation took over and gave too much of the responsibility of caring for a community to the federal government. Churches used to be the first line of defense in a community.

I believe we can give churches back this very important responsibility. Give churches the freedom and opportunity to again serve their communities in the ways they see fit. Let them feed the hungry and clothe the naked, as the Bible calls for, with no governmental intrusion.

But this doesn't mean simply trading one piece of welfare for another by doing away with a federal program that gives free money to welfare-bound recipients only to have churches or community groups turn around and give these same people free money or resources. No, the answer is more complex than that. No person who has become dependent on welfare can truly be free if allowed to continue to receive something for free. The key is to help the person realize the beauty of self-reliance by building into the program some measure by which the person has to contribute in order to receive.

Each local community can decide the best way to address these issues.

One such organization addressing these issues is Love INC. Love INC is a faith-based, non-profit organization serving the needs of communities. This organization, made up of church affiliates across the country and elsewhere, helps those in need through the use of donations and volunteer time and assistance.

"It's always been a personal goal of mine to be focused on something Christ-centered," said Tammy Boushek, executive director of Love INC of Douglas County Lakes Area Minnesota.

"We have volunteers here two to three hours a day," Boushek said. "A client will be referred to us by social services, a church, a friend, another organization, etc., so when someone calls in, we have a process that the volunteer starts a file on that person, it's called an intake."

After the person in need goes through the intake process and certain information is verified, Love INC sees how best to help, using program resources or referring the person to a church for assistance.

Love INC has three levels of affiliate relationships, including clearinghouses that link those in need with services, relational ministries that meet the deeper needs of individuals and families through mentoring, and comprehensive community development that spreads throughout the community.

Boushek said affiliates that have formed the deeper relationships with communities through relational ministries and community development have seen long-term changes in those areas with residents coming off public assistance and becoming self-sufficient. "The affiliates that have established and accomplished this model have seen statistically where people are no longer needing to utilize welfare; they are budgeting on their own. So it really is life-changing when you reach that model."

The change comes because of the deep involvement of the faith-based organization. "When someone needs help with the financial piece and a mentor comes along and takes the person's checkbook for an entire year, helping them promote a plan with the power of prayer and seeing how those prayers are answered, that creates change," Boushek said, as education and the support of a church family come together to help lift the recipient out of dire circumstances. "Through that, they are encouraged and see hope."

Love INC funding comes through churches, individual donors, some grants, and fundraisers. Some churches include Love INC as a line item in their budgets. Others provide donations. "We've had success with private donors, so we've just dipped into fundraising," Boushek said. "Just this year, we have budgeted for fundraisers. We have an annual garage sale. We have a Christian music concert that brings in $1,000 or so. And our large fundraiser, a live auction, is something we are hoping will be our signature event."

The funding that goes to the organization, whether from churches, other organizations, or fundraisers, is an example of how faith-based groups can help their communities.

While Love INC is a faith-based organization, it doesn't require those who call for help to attend church or participate in religious activities. Volunteers offer prayer, and many of those who seek assistance do accept it.

Boushek said her local affiliate served 131 adults and 146 children in the first quarter of 2012, with a total of 463 needs met. Needs included furniture, clothing, etc. Her affiliate has about 500 volunteers in its database and relationships with 31 churches.

That organization helps hundreds of people, right there locally. And it does a better job than the federal government. How much government bloat could we remove if we let local communities meet the needs of their residents?

CHAPTER 8

The Connection Between Social & Economic Issues

Social changes over the past 50 years have turned families upside down. Some changes, such as legalization of abortion, had an immediate impact, while others, such as governmental programs to act as a safety net for families in need, have eroded the family structure over time and have created generations of families dependent on governmental assistance.

A call for fathers to stand up

One of the most far-reaching social changes is the basic structure of the family. In fact, there is a very big social change going on right now in relation to how we raise children. Having a child out of wedlock is no longer taboo nor does it even raise a question today. Our society has so crumbled that we've come to a point where fathers actually seem optional. More and more young women are choosing or accepting to have children without the benefit of marriage.

It is now a fact that most pregnancies to women under 30 years of age occur outside of marriage.[4] This new trend directly impacts all of us. It used to be something limited mostly to poor women and minorities, but Middle America has embraced this. Women who have been raised in conservative homes in the Midwest, the Bible Belt, and other places you wouldn't expect to see this, are now a part of this trend. No longer is marriage a prerequisite for having children or even a preference.

It would be easy to lay blame at the feet of these women, but as a man, I believe I must first call upon men and fathers to do better by their families.

As I was thinking about America's youth, I stopped for a short visit with a Willmar tough guy Bob Poe — promoter of one of the largest youth-family Christian music festivals in Minnesota, Sonshine. He also is the director of West

---

[4] DeParle, Jason. For women under 30, most births occur outside marriage. (February 17, 2012). New York Times. Retrieved from http://www.nytimes.com/2012/02/18/us/for-women-under-30-most-births-occur-outside-marriage.html

Central Minnesota Youth for Christ. To visit with Bob one-on-one is a difficult thing to do for most of us men because it is a struggle to fight the tears as you listen to Bob's cry for America's youth. No question, we have failed our youth. And it is us — fathers who have failed, as our hearts for our children have grown cold. Youth for Christ is engaged in a heroic battle to be "for every kid ... one at a time." As I left Bob, he stopped me cold on my way out and asked: "Lee, what does the last verse say in the Old Testament?"

I looked at Bob and said, "I honestly cannot tell you."

Bob grinned, "Well what about the first verse?"

I said, "In the beginning God created the heaven and the earth."

Bob nodded and said, "Yes most people get the first verse, but very few remember the last verse."

Bob then pulled out the old book of wisdom and read from Malachi 4:6:

"He will turn the hearts of the parents to their children, and the hearts of the children to their parents; or else I will come and strike the land with total destruction."

Bob's point and my conclusion is not that an "angry" God intentionally will act through time and space to punish America. God does not need to punish us. Nature's law itself will provide the reckoning as we now face a generation of youth in America who have been neglected, ignored, not molded, not encouraged, and not loved by their fathers. Is there hope? Yes, but it must start at home — in the heart of the fathers.

As a married father myself of three boys, who now are teenagers or young men, I reflect over the difficulties we had as a family to raise strong and independent children in a culture of entitlements — yet with declining prosperity as the largeness of government is stifling freedom and economic opportunities. It is no wonder that I see less "fire" in the eyes of today's youth compared to my friends from when I came back to America as a young man in the early 1980's. As a father I have high expectations from my children because each child is wired by the Creator with talents to bless others. But it has become very difficult in our culture to create an environment that is helpful for our children to discover that it takes more than talent to succeed. Enduring success requires grueling work to hone skills, a servant attitude to fill a larger market potential, and a willingness to overcome obstacles.

We must admire and respect the many single mothers and grandmothers who nevertheless have successfully managed to raise their children by themselves. In the middle of demanding careers as single mothers or as grandmothers who stepped in for a generation of fathers which forfeited its responsibility, they gave everything in order to feed, teach, and encourage the coming generation. No doubt, many children grew up as wonderful and successful citizens from these circumstances. These single mothers and grandmothers therefore take offense, and rightfully so, when others deem their circumstances as detrimental.

For the love of children and the survival of America, we must however dare to expand into this issue of single parenthood. We cannot afford to not engage on this issue and must reject the constraints which political correctness imposes on our society.

Government assistance
factor in family breakdown

Our society is breaking down on several levels today, which seems to justify policymakers' tendency to implement policies and regulations to dictate behavior.

But I believe the policies contribute to the breakdown, rather than address or fix it. One such example is that of welfare. When the government insists on taking on the role of financial provider for a family, it undermines families and family values. When a mother finds that she can get money for her children and herself if the father is not around, then she is inclined to look to the government to do so, rather than the father.

As a result, many children grow up in one-parent homes because governmental policies encourage such a family structure. While I know many single parents are hard-working and raise children who become healthy, happy, and productive members of society, I also know that it is better for children to be raised in loving, two-parent households. This is not about passing judgment on the individuals who are single parents, but about looking at the circumstances related to single parenting and issues affecting children.

A single-parent household increases the likelihood that a child will grow up poor. Marriage reduces that likelihood. Nearly 40% of single-parent, female-led households with children are poor, but when you introduce marriage into the equation, you find that less than 7% of married, two-parent families with children are poor.[5]

Welfare, originally intended to help families going through a rough patch, has turned into a way of life for many and as such, has become the preferred means of support. This governmental program not only contributes to the breakdown of the family by encouraging single-parenthood, but it also contributes to poverty. It actually makes the recipients more dependent on a system that says it is there to help them!

This dependency then turns into a tool that keeps families in poverty. So a social program to help families actually has a negative economic impact. But this doesn't affect only the families taking the assistance. It affects every one of us as Americans. That is because we have to pay for it through taxation. Welfare spending is expected to cost us — yes, you and me — $10.3 trillion by 2020.[6]

These programs are tearing our families apart and causing tremendous harm to our society. The breakdown of the American family — encouraged by government programs — is a dire example of how social and economic issues converge.

[5] Rector, Robert. Marriage: America's greatest weapon against child poverty. September 16, 2010. Heritage Foundation. Retrieved from http://www.heritage.org/research/reports/2010/09/marriage-america-s-greatest-weapon-against-child-poverty

[6] Solutions for America: the unsustained growth of welfare. August 17, 2010. Heritage Foundation. Retrieved from http://www.heritage.org/research/reports/2010/08/the-unsustainable-growth-of-welfare

In addition to the fact that children born to single parents are more likely to be poor, it's also true that those children have an increased likelihood of becoming involved in illicit and illegal activities. The most vulnerable of those, the at-risk children living in poverty in single-parent homes, are more likely to repeat the cycle. That means they will grow up to themselves become welfare parents, with few prospects and no will to do better.

Social programs destroy feeling of family, community

Social programs have another consequence, and that is that they encourage a focus on self. And while a healthy concern for the individual is good, when we become so focused on self to the exclusion of service to others, we run into problems. America, even from its beginning, was never just about self, for in America, value of the individual self finds purpose in serving others. That is an American concept because America was the only nation in modern history that proclaimed that we exist because of unalienable rights. Because it was the Creator who gave us life and we were created with a purpose, to be self-sufficient and capable of self-government. That gave a higher value to the individual in America compared to any other nation where people were numbers or they were a part of a social group or a class. Someone ruled over them and gave them value that could be taken.

But in America, because our rights came from our Creator, that is the optimal value. If you as an individual become too self-focused, then you will individually limit how much value you can provide.

Everything we do in life is really for the benefit of other people. Anything that we produce or do has value because other people make it valuable. Our individual strengths become valuable when we use them to serve some portion of the whole.

That is the beauty of free enterprise.

When we have a strength and we use it to produce something others have deemed valuable, then we are rewarded for that.

People who feel entitled to receive certain goods and services even though they have done nothing to earn them or have made no contribution to the society to help produce them do not feel a sense of responsibility to contribute. This is yet another result of governmental interference through social programs. When people feel no responsibility to contribute or be productive, then their families and communities suffer.

But that's not all.

Social changes redefine life

We know that life, liberty, and the pursuit of happiness are dear to us all. But social changes over the last four decades have sought to try to redefine the very idea of life. As Christians, we know that every life is precious, and no amount of judicial activism or governmental can make us believe otherwise.

Liberal thinking now has made abortion the law of the land by turning this very serious Christian issue into merely a question of what a woman does with her body. But taking the life of another — in this case, an unborn child — ceases to be about a woman's body and becomes about killing. In no other context are we so apt to say it is all right to take a life. So why would we do the same with a child? Is it because that child hasn't been born and has no voice? That can't be.

We must be that child's voice.

The Bible states clearly that "thou shalt not kill," and we can't be so brazen as to think we can rewrite it for our own convenience.

But it's not just the moral issue. Abortion is normally seen as a social issue — and it is — but it has far-reaching economic implications, as all social issues do. Some tallies estimate abortions since 1970 have cost the U.S. economy $35 trillion in lost productivity and tax revenue in the form of the 50.5 million aborted babies who were never born to become productive citizens.[7]

Can you imagine for a moment how different our country would be if those babies' lives had been valued enough to be spared? We could have prosperity that we can't even imagine right now. Our local communities may not have had to face some of the serious issues they have had to face, including poorly funded schools, shortages of doctors and nurses, and streets and roads in disrepair.

And what about the untold, untapped potential? One of those aborted babies may have given us the cure for cancer or even the common cold. That is the economic impact of abortion.

This is what happens when government interferes in personal lives.

Too much government equals average — or worse

Governmental interference doesn't stop at forcing entitlement programs on us that we don't need and that are actually detrimental. And it doesn't stop at redefining our values and basic understandings of life. It also erodes our achievement.

A big push in education has been that of standardization. Standardized tests are said to help our children perform better.

But when you go for standardization across the land, you will get average.

Standardization plays to the most common denominators, with no regard to the best decisions. In education, for

---

[7] Ertelt, Steven. Researcher: abortions cost economy $35 trillion since 1970 in lost productivity. October 13, 2008. Lifenews.com. Retrieved from http://lifenews.com/2008/10/13/nat-4440

instance, standardization has resulted in an educational system that has our children coming out at the middle or bottom without earning a list of achievements.

Does this mean American children are unintelligent?

Of course not. But what it does mean is that the American education system is too weighted down by standardization according to some false idea of national academic regulations that it cannot allow individual communities to educate their children in the best way for them.

We no longer let parents and local communities decide what is best. Now, schools are forced to adhere to standardization requirements that have no bearing on reality.

This is no way for America to prepare the next generation to lead. It's a recipe for mediocrity.

Standardized tests force local schools to ensure students memorize facts to pass tests based on standards Washington bureaucrats deem fit rather than focus on learning concepts to become productive, thinking adults.

How can we expect to compete in the world when our government refuses to allow our children to truly learn?

When you compare American student achievement to that of other major industrialized nations, as counted in the Group of Eight (G8), American student achievement is lacking in key areas. The U.S. average math score was lower than that of Japan, Canada, Germany, and France, and not very different from that of the United Kingdom and Italy.

Of the eight nations, the U.S. average score was only higher than that of the Russian Federation.[8]

In science, U.S. students did not fare much better, as the average American science literacy score was lower than the average of Japan, Canada, Germany, and the UK, without much difference from average scores in France. The U.S. average was higher than the average in Italy and the Russian Federation.

With performance like this in key areas like math and sci-

---

[8] National Center for Education Statistics, Institute of Education of Sciences. (2011). Comparative indicators of education in the United States and other G-8 countries: 2011.

ence, what does the future hold for American students and for us as a whole? For it is the students we are educating today who will lead tomorrow. If we are not preparing them to compete, what results can we expect?

American education has changed since the founding of this nation. Because of the emphasis on standardized testing, more and more school systems and teachers feel pressure to "teach to the test," which is the act of teaching what is most likely to be on the test, rather than teaching a broad range of topics within a subject.

This reduces a child's likelihood to be able to apply a concept to a practical situation and it also makes for a shallow depth of knowledge within a particular subject area. American students spend less time in school and on homework than students in many other nations, so the focus on educational achievement may not be as strong as it once was.

I am a firm believer that local communities can do a better job educating their children when given the freedom to do so. Let's return education to the local community and help our students get to the head of the pack.

CHAPTER 9

Healing Healthcare

Healthcare as we know it is endangered in America. We're at such a critical point that what we do right now will determine the fate of millions of Americans and will determine the health of our nation for generations to come.

The most detrimental healthcare legislation our country has ever seen is being implemented over the next few years. It is the mission of an ultra-liberal president and could take us to a European-style healthcare system that is marked by excessively long wait times for care and high taxation.

First, do no harm

The healthcare legislation, called Patient Protection and Affordable Care Act or, more commonly, Obamacare, that we are discussing as the most recent example of governmental overreaching even goes so far as to infringe on our religious liberties by requiring healthcare plans to offer certain "family planning" services known as contraception. The legislation forces Americans to purchase health insurance, and then forces health care plans to offer contraceptives that may be against the moral beliefs of many in the faith community. This is just one of many examples from the healthcare legislation that demonstrates how governmental interference impinges upon our personal liberty and undermines personal responsibility.

The larger our government becomes, the more this country falls into decline, as we get more and more away from what our country was intended to be. Large government turns us into something our founding fathers would not even recognize, were they alive today.

Medical students are taught the concept of "first, do no harm," in medical school. It is the idea that they must consider the negative impact or possible harm any intervention they do can have. And if that risk is greater than the certainty of benefit, they should consider refraining from the intervention action.

Those who backed the healthcare reform would have done well to consider this same principle, "first, do no harm." For the harm this healthcare legislation will bring to our country far outweighs any modest benefit. Dismantling our healthcare system will cause significant harm, including a permanent loss of economic activity, weakening of our nation's fiscal strength, and a loss of quality of life for individuals and families.

Small business creates most jobs in America. Yet, Obamacare will impose stiff taxes that will hurt small business, the country's job creators. One such tax will be a 2.3 percent excise tax levied on the gross sale of medical devices. According to the Wall Street Journal, companies with tight margins could be taxed out of business.[9] This could take the profit out of a small, cash-strapped business, turning the free enterprise pursuit of economic opportunity into a government-burdened failed endeavor.

Repealing Obamacare isn't just about keeping our healthcare system, but it's also about rejecting a burdensome tax increase and protecting jobs.

This is not to suggest that we don't need to fix healthcare. We have the best healthcare system in the world, but it does have problems — many of which would not be remedied by more governmental interference. The problems are not because of the failure of our free-market system, but can be attributed to a combination of factors: an aging population, slowing economy, disappointing results from the managed care approach, and restricted competition due to governmental regulations and taxation. Taxation that targets small businesses and regulations that prevent such actions as the interstate sale of health insurance make real competition and quality improvements difficult.

Looking simply at healthcare spending is an incomplete view of whether our healthcare system has a problem. We spend 10 times more today on healthcare than we did in

---

[9] Improvised explosive device tax. (2012, May 28). The Wall Street Journal. Retrieved from http://online.wsj.com/article/SB10001424052702303610504577420583641142426.html

1950, according to The Heartland Institute.[10] That would suggest that costs are out of control and we are on a dangerous path. But if you look at why we spend so much, then you'll see it's a much different picture. There are a few reasons we spend more on healthcare now than we did more than 60 years ago.

One, we work harder to prolong lives. As an example, we spend more on saving premature infants and extending the lives of our elderly, a contrast to some other countries that may not put as much into prolonging the lives of the most vulnerable. That increases the amount spent on healthcare. So one reason we spend more is because we do more for our sick.

Another reason we spend more money on healthcare today is because more goes into treatments, care, and services that were not even available not so long ago. So advances in medicine have meant more dollars have gone into healthcare spending.

These are good reasons to spend money on healthcare, giving individuals along with their doctors the decisions on the best course of treatment or care. That's what happens when government regulations do not interfere. But when government gets involved in healthcare, there is a risk that certain lifesaving treatments and care might not be offered — even if they are available.

Healthcare that works

That's what concerns Nick Zerwas. He was born with tricuspid atresia, which meant he was born with a three-chambered heart. He has undergone ten open-heart surgeries. Doctors said he would live to maybe age seven. He is now 31. He attributes his survival to faith, family, and excellent healthcare. He said Obamacare or efforts to provide

---

[10] Heartland Institute releases ten principles of healthcare policy. (2007, September 26). The Heartland Institute. Retrieved from http://heartland.org/press-releases/2007/09/26/heartland-institute-releases-ten-principles-health-care-policy

universal healthcare will take medical care in this country in the wrong direction, especially for individuals with serious health issues.

"What universal healthcare does in nearly all societies is takes a standardized, mediocre level of care and applies it to everybody with cost limiting and care limiting models," he said. "When you provide healthcare free to all, you can only do it to a standard level, to a standard patient. What's difficult is that there are almost no standard patients and that's what ends up being a limiting force. A standardized healthcare system does not have room for experimental surgeries to the extent they are needed to extend life."

Experimental surgeries helped give him the life he has today.

"After the (Supreme Court's decision to uphold the Affordable Care Act), I'm afraid. I am afraid at what this means for other people with serious issues and eventually I'm afraid for what it means for me. I am hard-pressed to see ten years from now where they take a 41- or 42-year-old man who has lived his life six, seven times past the expectancy and they tell my wife, we've done all we can."

He doesn't want to have his medical decisions left up to some government-run healthcare system that doesn't see the benefit in spending more money on a middle-aged man with a delicate health situation. Zerwas said a healthcare system built on a standard of basic care will not be able to accommodate people with special health needs, especially as they get older.

His concerns stem from his own experience. Zerwas spent his childhood in and out of hospitals undergoing risky and experimental heart surgeries. He had two surgeries early in life to try to correct his heart ailment, with other surgeries as he got older. "When I was 7, I was a first-grader," he said. "My lips were blue because I didn't get enough oxygen. I was the smallest kid in my class. I didn't have enough energy to walk up a flight of stairs."

Doctors performed an experimental heart surgery on him in 1987 that had failed the year before on a six-year-old girl.

He was the first patient to survive that particular experimental surgery in Minneapolis. He later had other surgeries.

When he was in his teens, Zerwas was white-listed for a heart transplant. He waited two-and-a-half years for a match but they didn't find one. Doctors discharged him from the hospital without much hope, telling him there wasn't much else they could do.

"Go home and spend that time with your family," Zerwas recalled the words of the doctors, as they told him he had only a few months left to live.

"During that time period when I was waiting for the heart transplant in the hospital, I was tested for over 1,000 different donor hearts," Zerwas said. "I had an elevated antibody level, because of all the different surgeries. So they tested me and it kept coming back, no match."

He describes the hope of anticipating a new heart and the disappointment of realizing it was not to be: "They'd put me to sleep, and I'd wake up with my chest cracked open with no new heart. I was 15 years old, and I lost faith."

Tired of the disappointment and not seeing how it could get better, he mustered the energy to get out of bed one day. "I made a sign with a Magic Marker that said 'Do not enter, no nurses, no doctors, no family.' I taped it to my door and turned off all the lights. For the next couple of days anytime someone walked through the door, I just started screaming. 'Get out!' I didn't want to see anyone. I was done. I quit."

He recalled that time. "After a few days of doing that, I was asleep and my door swung open. I was kind of groggy. I started to say 'leave me alone.' It was my mom. She grabbed me by the scruff of the neck and pulled my butt out of bed. She was crying and hysterical. She was screaming, 'No, you can't! You can't give up on me. For 15 years, I didn't give up on you. You sure as hell aren't going to give up on me.'"

Zerwas continued: "She said, 'Nick, most of our life has been around getting you here and through this. You cannot give up. If we try everything and it doesn't work, I can accept that. But if you give up and stop fighting, I can never forgive you.' That was the kick in the butt I needed. Yes, I was upset, but it wasn't only about me."

There was a family, a church community, and others who had been praying with and for Zerwas for 15 years.

A few months later, Nick underwent another surgery. His health has continued to improve and today he leads an active life. He and his wife recently celebrated their seventh wedding anniversary. He is on the Elk River City Council, a city about 34 miles northwest of Minneapolis. He is running for Minnesota House of Representatives. He believes in service and is grateful for the life he has today.

It scares him to think a healthcare mandate could take that opportunity away from a child born with similar ailments today. "My life is an example of why you never stop believing and you never give up hope."

Saving babies, the sick, and others with delicate health is not a bad way to spend money. But as we move away from the close relationship between a doctor or other healthcare provider and the patient, we go to a system that engenders a closer relationship between the doctor and the insurance company, making the insurance companies the doctors' customers, and not their patients. In such a case, patients aren't even given all the necessary information to make informed decisions about their care, often because the options aren't even available because they have been deemed unnecessary or inappropriate in decisions made by people other than the patients and their doctors.

The reason to include the story of Nick Zerwas is to point out that the very point in which we permit government to assign someone other than you to determine who shall have a chance to live or not, what kind of health care service to receive or not, that is the point in which America ceases to be America. That is the point in which "life, liberty and the pursuit of happiness" changes from God to you and reassigned from you to government. The downside to government-run health care is that eventually someone who is not you must decide what your life is worth. Those who are weak, the very young, and/or the older generation, and those who require more complex, more risky and costlier health care services, will by definition "earn" less net contributable value to society compared to someone in the "prime" of their life. This ideology is a dangerous proposition when backed by the force of government determining the worth of your life.

In contrast, when you and your family are in total control of what to do with your life, what health care services to seek or not seek, what you can afford or not afford, then we do not need to be afraid of being denied our unalienable right to life. Nick's mother fought for his life. She was not ready to give up, would not forgive Nick if he stopped fighting for his life, and could not release him to the good Lord until they had done all they could do.

Nick and his mother "danced" and "fought" for life. Nick's doctors invented new and risky procedures to save his life. The government had no play in this fight for life. The overall cost incurred in our society to pay for Nick's operations are nothing compared to the value Nick and others like him are providing for America. Our way of "life, liberty and pursuit of happiness" allowed this young boy from Elk River the opportunity to become a braveheart, an American hero.

We currently are moving toward a new health care system to be controlled by government and which eventually will evolve into a "universal" health care system. This system will then require expert groups to develop directives to be followed when making health care decisions. The aim becomes to allocate what the system sees as limited health care resources amongst the people. As we then become a society where someone other than you measures the value of the individual life in terms of age, economic contribution and the probability for survival, we then deny ourselves the opportunity to become what we can become. We will forfeit the unique stories of conquest over death and the defeats by death. These stories inspire others to accomplish extraordinary accomplishments for our nation.

The gain to America from Nick's survival has far more value to our nation than can be directly measured as attributable to his own labor and time on earth. In America we celebrate, we hope, we gain courage, when "underdogs" like

Nick cut through the harsh difficulties of life. The value that Nick provides as an encouragement to others is beyond direct measurable economics. How can government or any expert measure what value Nick will provide to society through his inspirational story when told to other people facing handicaps or to "average" people who can do much better? If Nick can do it, if he can be a champion in life, if he can overcome his obstacles, then so can you.

The American way is when people inspire and challenge each other to do much more. We thus become the most productive people in the world. America will forfeit its national character if we begin to deny Nick and others the opportunity to become heroes. As we through our human struggle overcome difficulties and life-threatening circumstances, we create gems of blessings and inspirations for others to become better versions of themselves.

Obama's health care reform is therefore a direct challenge to the American framework of who we are as a people. Are we as Americans endowed with an inalienable right to life from our Creator or is government the rights giver and arbitrator of such rights? You know the answer.

Where our healthcare system needs improvement

The Heartland Institute[11] concludes it is easy to identify waste and inefficiencies in all segments of our healthcare system, from hospitals to government programs, to private insurance. It points to the lack of transparency in healthcare pricing, number of people who lack health insurance, and the high rate of medical mistakes made at hospitals, among others. The solution to this goes back to our free market, because patients — not insurance companies — should be

---

[11] Bast, Joseph L. Ten principles of health care policy. The Heartland Institute.

the doctors' customers. The solution is to again make the relationship between doctor and patient the relationship that counts. It's only when doctors see patients as their customers that the doctors will be free to give the best advice to their patients. This will also mean doctors will be free to provide to patients information necessary to make informed decisions.

Taking this course will increase the supply of quality care and reduce the cost of that care. Taking the time to address these individual issues will provide a much better benefit than can ever come from the "sledgehammer" approach Obamacare offers. We do not need further mandates, government regulations, and medical panels to stand between us and quality healthcare. That is not the way to improve our healthcare system.

The free market is the best arbiter because it will reduce cost and improve care. We already see its effect in the case of elective services that are not covered by health insurance plans. There, costs for such elective services as Lasik eye surgery and cosmetic surgery have declined because the free market is allowed to play out — providers compete freely and patients (consumers) spend their own money. If a medical facility or physician doesn't do a great job, patients will take their money elsewhere.

Why we cannot afford Obamacare

One of the issues Obamacare is said to address is that of free riders who refuse to purchase health insurance. Their care is then subsidized by others when they receive emergency room treatment. But there are a few problems with certain assumptions about those without health insurance. Yes, there are some people who do not pay insurance premiums because of economic misfortunes, including job loss and low wages. And some don't pay because they refuse to accept responsibility for their care. But many young people do not pay premiums because they simply refuse to subsidize premiums for others, including older Americans. Obamacare doesn't address the reasons people go without health insurance, yet it tries to have it both ways by extending coverage and sweetening the benefit package through the use of mandates and broad coverage.

Obamacare promises that Americans will receive more healthcare and spend less, but that's simply a promise it can't deliver. And current purchasers of health insurance won't simply stand by as they are forced to subsidize everybody else. Some employers, especially small businesses that employ between 50 and 100, said they would consider dropping health coverage for employees, under Obamacare.[12]

But dropped coverage isn't the only concern facing Americans in coming years. The Association of American Medical Colleges estimates that America will face a shortage of 45,000 or more primary care physicians by 2020, with that number increasing to more than 90,000, when you count surgeons and specialists.[13] What's even scarier is that more than 80 percent of physicians said they have considered quitting, and may do so under Obamacare.[14]

Obamacare will punish doctors by increasing their workloads and lowering their compensation.

Most of these doctors won't quit outright, but a high number will. Some will switch career paths and go into other less restrictive and more financially rewarding work, while those providers who are in their 50s and 60s will retire earlier than otherwise because of the intrusion they see coming from further government regulations. And young people who once considered entering the medical field, will evaluate other occupations that have less onerous regulations and restrictions.

The combined effect of forcing coverage to more

[12] Rogers, Kate. (2012, July 24). Survey finds Obamacare means nearly 10% of businesses to drop coverage. Fox Small Business Center. Retrieved from http://smallbusiness.foxbusiness. com/legal-hr/2012/07/24/survey-finds-obamacare-means-nearly-10-businesses-to-drop-coverage

[13] AAMC. Physician shortages to worsen without increases in residency training. Retrieved from https://www.aamc.org/download/286592/data/physicianshortage.pdf

[14] Doctor Patient Medical Association. Doctors' attitudes on the future of medicine. http://www.doctorsandpatients.org/resources/85-physician-attitudes-survey-june-2012

people and the anticipated decline in the number of medical providers is why I call Obama's healthcare reform the "sledgehammer."

Obamacare will increase cost, reduce the quality of healthcare, drive physicians out of the field, increase unemployment, and speed up America's decline. This is all avoidable if we succeed in creating a movement to restore America to its original principles of limited federal government and free enterprise.

That is the true picture of what awaits us under Obamacare.

While some will find hope in Obamacare, many others will find themselves as losers. Transforming our healthcare into a government-run system will be catastrophic. If there is any doubt, then it only requires a look at the numbers. They speak for themselves, and they are mind-boggling. Obamacare includes 12 forms of tax hikes that will affect families earning less than $250,000 per year, as well as $525 billion in new taxes, fees, and penalties on families and small business. It will cost America over $1.76 trillion over the next 10 years.[15]

This is just one step toward the implementation of a European-style universal healthcare system that overtaxes us and under delivers. That is what this is about, and it is what we must fight against now. This struggle is not about being Democrat or Republican. This is about if we believe that a central government is better able to run your life or if you have it in you to be self-governed?

Is this really what we want?

Absolutely not. We do not want to lose the strength of our American healthcare system with its much better individualized attention and replace it with something that does not work.

---

[15] The real deal on healthcare repeal. The Daily Statesman. Retrieved from http://www.dailystates man.com/blogs/1595/entry/48601/

Solutions to fix healthcare

The solutions to fix our healthcare system and which will benefit our overall economy must be a combination of the following steps/principles:

• Recognize that price controls lead to shortages. When government sets fees, often below the true cost of the provided service, it creates a shortage of treatment that is needed by the people. We should move to gradually remove such price controls.

• Recognize that competition reduces prices. Again, consider the Lasik eye surgery and cosmetic surgery as an example of where competition and innovation provide a better service, at a lower cost, and for more people.

• Recognize that people respond to price signals and increased cost sharing.

Reduce regulations and enhance competition:

• Mandated benefits, which are usually promoted as being "pro-consumer," actually increase cost, reduce innovation, reduce choice, and over time reduce quality. Eliminations of such mandates combined with new laws to allow individuals to purchase insurance across state lines will reduce cost and improve quality through increased interstate competition.

• Employer-provided health insurance is paid using before-tax dollars while individual healthcare policies are not tax deductible. We should also allow individual policies to be tax deductible as such will increase options, increase insurance coverage, and reduce cost. Growing individual policies will reduce over-reliance on third-party payers and reduce over-all cost as people will manage their cost better for the services they need through direct payment.

• Reduce overall cost to insurance premiums by capping noneconomic damages in medical malpractice lawsuits.

• Allow individuals, farmers, and small businesses to form purchasing pools.

• Allow Health Saving Accounts to use funds for insurance premiums.

• Prevent discrimination against individuals with pre-existing conditions who maintain continuous coverage.

• Amend laws to allow individuals who wish to switch from one plan to another with the same protections.

• Allow employers to change their healthcare benefits from outdated defined-benefit model to a defined-contribution model.

• Overall concept: expand consumer choice, enable portability of individual coverage, remove barriers of competition in both the private and public sectors.

CHAPTER 10

Heartland Issues in Agriculture Will Play a Key Part

"There's never been a time when production agriculture has been more successful, and yet under more threat."

— Mike Yost, Swift County Minnesota farmer and former USDA Foreign Agricultural Service Administrator

Agriculture is a cornerstone of the economic well-being and way of life in Minnesota, and in particular, Minnesota's 7th Congressional District. Minnesota ranks fourth nationally in crop cash receipts and seventh in livestock cash receipts, according to the Minnesota Department of Agriculture.[16] Minnesota farmers also play a significant and ever important role in helping feed a growing world population, with Minnesota being the sixth largest agricultural export state in the U.S.

Farmers in the 7th District have been blessed with great natural resources — productive soils, water availability, and transportation infrastructure to get products to market. The history of farming has always been about continuous improvement — innovation, research, utilization of new technology. Recent advancements in biotechnology, for example, have resulted in increased yields, producing more crops on fewer acres, and doing so in a more environmentally friendly manner.

Minnesota's farmers have both a moral obligation to feed the malnourished of the world and a tremendous economic opportunity to service a rapidly expanding global middle class. This window of opportunity is a gift from nature to Minnesota and fits with the productive character of our people. The opportunity is ours to go through. If we don't, farm-

---

[16] The real deal on healthcare repeal. The Daily Statesman. Retrieved from http://www.dailystates man.com/blogs/1595/entry/48601/

ers in other parts of the world will. While other countries are actively helping their producers, all we need is for the US government to stay out of the way.

Proposed regulations and activist activity will stifle growth

Our farmers in America are increasingly challenged with myriad new or proposed regulations, as well as challenges from activist groups, that if allowed to continue, will severely limit the ability of a new generation of farmers and ranchers to sustain and grow profitable farming operations, and threaten to put a chokehold on the economy and way of life for many in the 7th Congressional District and rural America at large.

There's always been a certain level of risk inherent in farming — weather, disease, markets, etc. However, today's risk and uncertainty increasingly comes from government rules or regulations and activist litigation. A few recent examples of government overreach, and activist threats include:

• Efforts by the EPA to regulate particulate matter (dust) on farms.[17]

• Efforts by EPA to greatly expand federal jurisdiction under the Clean Water Act — not through legislation, or rule-making, but through a "guidance document". The implications of this proposal would vastly increase EPA oversight and regulation of waters on farmland by eliminating the term "navigable" from the Clean Water Act.[18]

• A proposed U.S. Department of Labor (DOL) ruling regarding youth labor that would have severely limited youths' ability to participate directly in working in farming operations. As an example, the proposed rule would have prohibited youth 16 and under from operating power-driven

---

[17] The real deal on healthcare repeal. The Daily Statesman. Retrieved from http://www.dailystates man.com/blogs/1595/entry/48601

[18] EPA and U.S. Army Corps of Engineers Guidance Regarding Identification of Waters Protected by the Clean Water Act. [EPA-HQ-OW-2011-0409; FRL-9300-6].

equipment (including a battery powered screwdriver). After considerable pressure from agricultural interests, the DOL finally withdrew its proposed rule earlier in 2012.[19]

• Activist groups have filed litigation that would seek to severely limit or restrict the ability of farmers to access new biotechnology products (Roundup Ready Sugarbeets)[20] or current pesticide products (atrazine), even though these products already undergo rigorous USDA and/or EPA review before entering the marketplace.[21]

• Animal rights activist groups are also seeking to limit or eliminate certain animal husbandry practices — either through legislation, litigation, or by pressuring food companies not to purchase certain products deemed unacceptable — despite the fact that it's always been in the interest of livestock and poultry producers to care for their animals and use the best science and technology to do so.

The common theme running through all these issues? They all have the potential to restrict production practices, the introduction of new technologies, or add costs to farmers, and in doing so create uncertainty regarding the long-term competitiveness of Minnesota agriculture.

Agriculture is bright spot in economy

Agriculture has been one of the few positive spots in this economy. There's tremendous potential and opportunity for farmers into the future if they are allowed to do what they do best — grow and raise the food, feed, and fuel products in an efficient and safe manner that makes Minnesota and U.S. farmers the envy of the world.

There's a lot at stake, not just in Minnesota — but globally as well. According to the United Nations, global food production must double by 2050 in order to meet an ever increasing

---

[19] DOL Proposes Changes to Child Labor Rules on Farms. 54836 Federal Register. Vol. 76, NO. 171. September 2, 2011.

[20] Center for Food Safety et al v Charles Connor, acting secretary of USDA et al.

[21] City of Greenville, IL et al v Syngenta Crop Protection Inc and Syngenta Ag, case 3:10-cv-00188-jpg-pmf.

global population.[22] Minnesota farmers are ready to step up and help meet this challenge, if they are allowed to do so — if their government allows them to do so.

"Agriculture must continue to evolve," said Mike Yost, Swift County Minnesota farmer and former USDA Foreign Agricultural Service administrator. "We are all very proud of our history. In order to thrive and survive, we have to change and move forward. We can't have the government encumber us."

Food demand is growing

Yost said governmental resistance to changes and advances in technology makes it difficult for farmers to accommodate the food needs of their communities and the world. "If we can't use biotechnology and the new products that are in the pipeline that will be developed, we will not be able to meet that goal (of doubling production by 2050)."

U.S. farm exports were expected to total about $134.5 billion in fiscal year 2012, a $3.5 billion increase over the previous forecast.[23]

While drought threatened corn and soybean crops in particular in the summer of 2012, restrictive governmental regulations related to use of technology, animal husbandry, environmental factors, and other matters are bigger long-term dangers.

This is a shame because agriculture is one of the few bright spots in our nation's economy, as so many other sectors struggle.

[22] United Nations. (2009, October 9). Food production must double by 2050 to meet demand from world's growing population. Retrieved from http://www.un.org/News/Press/docs/2009/gaef3242.doc.htm

[23] USDA. (2012, May 31). Statement from agriculture secretary Vilsack on newest forecast for U.S. farm exports. Retrieved from http://www.usda.gov/wps/portal/usda/usdahome?contentid =2012/05/0173.xml&contentidonly=true

Biotechnology key to helping farmers meet food demand

Paul Aasness, 72 and a lifelong farmer, supports biotechnology that helps farmers improve crop yield and produce safe food, but he has seen opposition by some who do not understand or like genetic engineering in crops. Genetically engineered crops undergo rigorous testing before they are approved for commercial use and only those deemed safe are grown and put into the food supply. Genetic engineering in crops most often centers around virus, herbicide, and insect tolerance. Growing plants that can withstand herbicides, viruses, and insects helps boost crop output in any given year, as farmers can face devastating losses due to herbicide use, viruses, and insects.

"I can list many ways that biotech has helped me as a producer," Aasness said. "We have a choice to use them or not. But the administration is holding them back."

Poor understanding of biotechnology in agriculture causes fear in policy makers. But the fear is unfounded, as farmers aren't interested in products that would be unsafe to their lands or dangerous to humans, Aasness said. "Every farmer I know believes in sound science."

The opportunities we have to help meet the needs of a growing global population mean more jobs for Americans and more economic stability for American farmers and families. The future of agriculture is very good for another generation of farmers. But the downside is that if government and residents of large cities do not understand how all this comes about, they may make decisions or support actions to jeopardize the growth. Those actions by bureaucracy can overshadow the opportunities and the outcome will be disaster to the world if we cannot continue to enhance food production to meet the growing need.

We need leaders who understand heartland issues

Yost said some activist organizations have political and social agendas that, if successful, would damage livestock production. "We have groups that don't want livestock production and don't believe in consuming meat," Yost said. "They're working to promote ideas that will infringe on production practices."

Another issue is immigration, Yost said. "We have a hard time getting trained people to work on a farm, especially in livestock. The current immigration policy is confusing and ill-suited to our needs. We need to be able to at least bring in workers who can stay in the entire year or periods of years for all types of work, whether they come in as veterinarians, animal scientists, or pure workers to feed chickens and handle the animals."

The reality is that fewer and fewer Americans are connected to agriculture. They live in cities. Many have never been on a farm. Fewer and fewer people have parents and grandparents who own farms so the disconnect is growing. What happens is that because of the disconnect, these people do not know the issues facing agriculture and so they can be swayed or influenced by activists who would try to shape their opinions. Ultimately, that results in unfavorable public policies.

Aasness has seen the changes as fewer people have gone into farming. "Back in the early 70s, I built what at that time was a pretty large hog operation. I knew of a dozen farmers about my age who were doing a similar thing. Today, all of those ten or twelve farmers are no longer in business. Not because anyone forced them out but the families grew up and left."

The population is growing and so are people's expectations of the food they want. Those are long-term, structural changes that will require agriculture to be set free to do what it needs to do to deliver. Once regulation becomes excessive, it will drive out a new generation of American farmers. If they don't see the future in a reality where they can be free and do what they do well, we won't see that new generation of farmers and if that happens, you're talking about a huge negative consequence.

Aasness, a former member of the Minnesota state legislature, said it's necessary to have leaders who understand the challenges facing the Midwest and agriculture, as well as understand the benefits of such things as biotechnology in agriculture. They can facilitate policy discussions that help protect heartland interests. "We need leaders who will ask those questions."

Yost said, "I would argue that never in the history of the United States has production been more sustainable. There has never been more demand for our production. And it's never been so taxed. Whether it's the regulators, food safety advocates, or those wanting something to argue against."

Yost said what we do in the United States affects food supplies in other parts of the world. "From my travels in China, if those people do not have access to affordable food and a better diet, that government is going to be in trouble and consequently, the world is going to be in trouble economically and politically."

Another issue facing agriculture is availability of energy. High energy costs affect the bottom line. "I'm a believer in the biofuels but I am heavily dependent on fossil fuels," Aasness said. "I am a strong proponent of the development of fossil fuels. How are we going to sustain ourselves? How are we going to move our crops?"

He said we cannot abandon fossil fuels for biofuels. "Biofuels are like the teaspoon in the cup. But we have to keep the remainder of the cup."

If we don't address these heartland issues properly, the whole world will suffer.

CHAPTER 11

Winning Through Economics (America's Competitive Edge)

The United States is the world's only superpower. We reached there for several reasons, including the character of our people. The character of the American people became the nation's greatest asset. The American advantage is therefore more than its endless fields of agriculture or its boundless natural resources, but rather that America is the home of the most creative and productive people ever assembled. America remains a nation that is always expanding economic opportunities, pushing the frontier and welcoming new generations to advance through the various sectors of the economy. This mindset is embodied in the uniqueness of America's people and her entrepreneurs, and is what created America's competitive advantage.

The American Advantage

America's shared moral code and collective memory of traditions forged this competitive advantage as America coupled such attributes with individual work ethic, a drive to innovate, and unparalleled opportunity to enhance productivity through the free enterprise system. This led to what we know as American exceptionalism, or as we say in the Norwegian parts of Minnesota — making a reference to Garrison Keillor's fictional town of Lake Wobegon — a place where "all the children are above average."

Another way to describe the American advantage is through the concept of "speed of trust." As a self-governed people, with a moral code and a drive to pursue, the American people arose as a nation dedicated to economic prosperity for all people. The "speed of trust" is lived out daily in America by a people able to get along through its shared moral code and therefore able to engage in commerce without stifling governmental regulations. The process of maximizing economic and societal value thus became standard in America. Vetting of ideas, products, and services was left to the free market as the ultimate judge of value and fairness. This method of "checks and balances" as introduced by the American marketplace revolutionized the competitive realities of the world and America became second to none in efficiency and pursuit of opportunities. This American framework continues to serve as an unprecedented example of the free-market system. Speed of trust is essential.

In business or the creative process, what makes people, entrepreneurs, and investors come together and actually overcome challenges is having trust between the different partners. This allows you to break through much quicker and with much less stress.

For instance, if you have a team consisting of an entrepreneur, an inventor, an investor, and an engineer and they believe in each other and are told they don't need to worry about one taking advantage of the other, they will move forward much more quickly. They are not going to second-guess each other. They are going to take on challenges and be much stronger and get to market. But if you replace this team with people who don't trust each other, then it's likely they won't make it to market, or if they do, they will be much more inefficient and less effective than the first team. The speed of trust gives you economic advantage in taking an idea and bringing it to the marketplace for the benefit of society.

Holding on to the advantage

For generations, we have failed to teach morals and ethics and principles. We lose that advantage and we become like the rest of the world. The American advantage is that we were good, decent people who had morals and principles that brought us together. It allowed us to be more effective than nations who put regulations in place because there was the reality or perception that there wasn't enough trust. They needed the regulations because the trust was not there. But the problem is that you can't trust government either.

So then who is the best regulatory entity?

To me and those who believe in the free market, we believe the best mechanism to ensure goodness in what we do is the market itself. So if the market, which is the sum of all the people and all of the consumers, sees something that is deemed not beneficial, the market will not buy it. So the market itself will weed out those elements that do not fit.

The productive nature of the people striving for self-reliance is a measure of the goodness of the American people. The American story is not similar to any other comparable nation. America serves a higher purpose in history as it welcomed people from multiple nations and struggling circumstances to form one nation as "we the people."

When I came back to America in the late summer of 1982 after spending my childhood years in South America and Norway, I was struck by the uniqueness of my new American friends. These young Americans were different from the youths from the two other continents I had lived in before. My new friends had fire in their eyes to improve life through innovation, forged with iron in their wills to overcome obstacles, and born with love for freedom in their DNA as a guide for local solutions. After having lived in America from age 20 to approaching 50, it has become clear to me that these attributes of "fire, steel, and love" which I found in my American friends did not just happen by chance. I believe these attributes are the outcomes of values and principles passed on from generation to generation as the American culture.

No other county celebrates its flag as reverently as America. I believe there is a direct link between the American flag and the attributes I found in my American friends. The link goes back to America's Founding Fathers who "designed" the first American flag. After human history comprised thousands of years of struggle to attain freedom, a generation rose up with ideas ready to revolutionize the world with liberty. This generation as Founding Fathers of America found divine inspiration and wisdom within their collective group to declare: "We hold these truths to be self-evident, that all men are created equal, that they are endowed by their Creator with certain inalienable Rights, that among these are Life, Liberty and the pursuit of Happiness." This declaration spoke not only to the contemporaries, but served as a cry through the ages to both past and future generations, that the path to enduring freedom was finally discovered. Since this American Declaration of Independence, millions of people have joined the American dream and raised new generations of Americans dedicated to the same pursuit of life as a self-governed people. A year after the Declaration of Independence, the Founding Fathers 'designed' the first American flag in 1777 with 13 stars. The stars didn't just symbolize the 13 colonies, but something grander: they called it a new constellation.

The symbols represented by the colors in the American flag are not arbitrary, but serve as an explanation for why I could still sense "fire, steal, and love" in America's youth two hundred years after America's formation.

The color red in the American flag is a symbol of hardiness and valor and is the steel I found in the willpower of my American friends. They were people Made in America to conquer obstacles.

The color blue in the flag is the symbol of vigilance, perseverance, and justice. The color blue is the fire I found in the eyes of my American friends. They had clarity to serve as protectors of what they believed in.

The color white in the flag is a symbol of purity and innocence. This attribute aligns each person with God and to each other. Through our love for God, nation, family, and freedom, we become more than a powerful nation and more than strong individuals. We strive for goodness as we accept the call to sacrifice for others. The color white is thus a symbol of goodness and the love I found in the hearts of my American friends.

Of these three attributes, red-steel-conqueror, blue-fire-protector, white-love-goodness, it is the color of white-love-and goodness which is the most important. These attributes of white and love connect the strength of fire and steel into something that is more than brute strength and is simply irresistible to any person who longs for liberty and meaning. The American Advantage thus became the combination of its limited federal government, the free enterprise system, and the character attributes of the American people.

The American government as a Center framework

Our American Founding Fathers crafted a fresh, unique, and revolutionary framework to encourage individual freedom, prosperity, and responsibility. This framework was based on Center principles — the truth that humankind is created free and is wired with proper training to become responsible beings. The principles from our Founding Fathers are timeless and represent a Center ideology that can be true for all generations. The relevance of this Center ideology is documented by history as humans continuously strive for freedom and find meaning in overcoming challenges (the pursuit of happiness). From this, I endeavor to declare that much of recent policies from both of our two primary political parties have trended left and will continue to trend left with increasing speed unless a new generation of leaders is called and willed into leadership by the people.

The American framework required a balanced ("Centered") approach for our nation to thrive. Each citizen and elected official should participate, regardless of party affiliation, in the process of balancing the "two wings of the American Political Eagle." These two wings are supposed to represent the force of conservation or force of compassion. If either wing dominates, it will lead to either anarchy or tyranny. Although it seems as if the wing of compassion only can do good, if left to dominate on its own, excessive or uncontrolled compassion will produce excessive cost and loss in individual drive to pursue.

It is this wing of "compassion" that has not been controlled at the federal level and which will force our nation to crash land into fiscal bankruptcy. We have failed to measure each social program and/or distributive program by ignoring two tests: 1) Can we as taxpayers afford the cost of the programs and 2) will such programs reduce the well-being of our nation through deprived freedom and individual responsibility?

Today, nearly 50% of the American people live in households that receive some form of governmental assistance.[24] Although the U.S. government historically has been reluctant to absorb ownership of free market assets, current political and economic circumstances have resulted in public ownership of substantial production assets. These bailouts and additional social programs can only be financed through additional taxation, additional borrowing (to be paid as debt by future generations) or by printing of new money (plundering from current generation through inflation). The end result of more welfare or increasing socialism is usually conflict and forced redistribution between generations and/or the classes: the productive versus less productive or rich versus poor. The ultimate loss of excessive "compassionate" programs is that it deprives the individual of self-worth that arises from overcoming challenges and brings tyranny from mandating official programs to each individual.

Thomas Jefferson anticipated that a time would come when our people may cease to live as a free people. Jefferson said, "The natural progress of things is for liberty to yield and government to gain ground."[25]

The true Center in American government

Unfortunately human nature is such that most of us try to label those we disagree with to fit a category. More often than not, such labeling falls short of describing the complexity and true nature of someone's opinion. Labeling is furthermore detrimental as labels usually are given without the proper historical and/or futuristic framework. Which generation throughout history is best positioned to

[24] Luhby, Tami. Government assistance expands. CNNMoney. Retrieved from http://money.cnn.com/2012/02/07/news/economy/government_assistance/index.htm

[25] Thomas Jefferson, The Works of Thomas Jefferson, Paul Leicester Ford, editor (New York and London: G.P. Putnam's Sons, 1905), Vol. V, to Edward Carrington, May 27, 1788

accurately assess if America's current policies are balanced at the Center, leaning to the right or leaning to the left? Perhaps it is impossible for any generation to judge itself fairly since it is human tendency for all to think: "I am balanced while others are not."

Unless we are willing to write-off the original and the Centered America that was anchored on liberty, individual responsibility, limited government, government for the people and by the people, and the pursuit of happiness and replace this original framework with a transformed America based on assimilation toward the European model and globalism, then I would state that perhaps the proper point of reference is to compare the various economic policies with the Center point as defined by our Founding Fathers. Note that as we move from the concept of Center government (limited government which Thomas Jefferson defined as good government), both the left and the right turn into a form of Statist "big" Government at the detriment of freedom and prosperity.

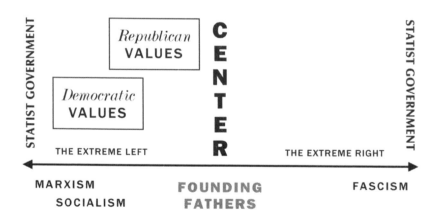

In the proper historical context, very few people should be classified as "extreme right." No question, we have deviated and moved to the left of America's true historical Center. The economic power and value creation that is possible is amazing when true Center-limited government and free-market policies are unleashed. I have lived on three continents and am believed to be fairly open-minded and versed in the various governance models. My life experience includes living in a totalitarian extreme right-wing dictatorship in South America, in the left leaning social democratic system of Norway, and in the historical center Republic of these United States of America. The framework crafted by our Founding Fathers for a government for the people and by the people and anchored on basic human rights endowed by the Creator is truly historical unique, brilliant, and advanced. Limited federal government is the most advanced governance system ever developed because it requires active participation by each citizen to seek optimal local solutions and is thus far superior to big government which in its simplistic nature requires assignment of individual responsibility to a federal bureaucracy.

A quick review of America's history shows that with about 5% of the world's population, America's limited federal government (Center) quickly created more wealth and opportunity than the rest of the world combined and has for more than a hundred years served as the food basket of the world. America can again shine as a free and strong nation if we adhere to Abraham Lincoln's call to "come back." President Lincoln urged his fellow Americans in 1858 to relearn the past: "(My) countrymen, if you have taught doctrines conflicting with the great landmarks of the Declaration of Independence, ... let me entreat you to come back; come back to the truths that are in the Declaration of Independence." The U.S. government was purposefully restricted from active interference in the affairs of the citizens. To this date, the early American experiment remains the longest continuous political-governance system in recorded history.

America must remain the leader of the free world to ensure continued freedom

America's economic strength has been under a gradual

domestic attack from creeping regulation and taxation. A significant cause of our declining economic freedom is furthermore attributable to the weakening of our shared moral code, the introduction of relativism, and the decline in the strength of the American family. These social factors have reduced the American competitive advantage through the decline in "speed of trust" and the individual drive to succeed. It is time we reject the erroneous and simplistic fallacy of "it's the economy, stupid." Loss in moral code and the increasing government are the two dual domestic destroyers of America's freedom and prosperity.

The world's global race for job opportunities is adding new challenges. For the sake of freedom and individual prosperity, it is vital that America remerges as the undisputed champion of free enterprise. The world is looking for solutions. These solutions will either be provided by nation(s) and system(s) which will represent various versions of centralized planning (such as the Chinese model) or by nations anchored on the principles of free enterprise and local decisions (the original American framework). The victorious solution provider will either increase or reduce freedom. We cannot trust the safeguarding of freedom to any other nation but to America. Why is America so vital in the safeguarding of freedom? The answer is simply that there is no other major nation or power (organization) wired in its character like America to uphold individual rights. Most nations apply a combination of rights provided by the power the State itself (Central Government), rights from a democratic majority, or rights from an elite group (secular and/or religious) in the process of allocating and restricting individual rights. As nations, organizations and/or groups expand their power and scope, such growth is more often than not at the detriment of individual rights and freedom. America, in contrast, is a republic, a nation that functions through basic laws and a limited government to protect such laws and rights.

Benjamin Franklin was asked at the close of the Constitutional Convention of 1787: "what have we got a republic or a monarchy?" Franklin answered, "A republic, if you can keep it." Although we are given liberty as unalienable rights from our Creator and thus cannot be deprived of our freedom by force from government and/or foreign power, we can lose our freedom if we elect to forfeit such liberty by choice.

How to measure America's journey to maintain freedom

Jim Clifton, chairman of the Gallup Organization, writes in The Coming Jobs War that 3 billion people want or are looking for work today but we have only 1.2 billion full-time jobs in the world.[26] His insightful view is that the future outlook of the world will not be defined by military or political power, but rather by which counties are best able to create jobs and grow GDP. The global GDP (Gross Domestic Product) is currently around $60 trillion. The United States accounts for about $15 trillion or 25 percent. The next 30 years will see the global GDP grow to $200 trillion. This competition for GDP growth is the battle of the future which will define winner and loser nations. America has no choice but to win this economic war because without a freedom-loving America there is no power sufficient enough to limit the control of intrusive governments. Clifton correctly explains that business drives everything – which is something many politicians in their lofty castles fail to understand.

What is the proper GDP target America should aim for to ensure continued freedom and prosperity? A common prediction by economists is that America "as is" will grow its GDP on average at about 2.5% over the next 30 years. The United States Congressional Office, for instance, predicts a growth rate of 2% for the future. The average GDP growth during the Obama presidency has been around 2.4%. These low GDP predictions and current realities are disasters in

---

[26] Clifton, Jim. (2011). The coming jobs war. Gallup Press.

the making. America will become a "has been nation" if we settle for leaders with wrong or no vision, with no or irrelevant experiences, and without strong leadership qualities that are essential to restore America's competitive advantage ("speed of trust"), limited government and free enterprise as our economic engine. Clifton warns if that happens China could dominate the world economically.

A world where China is the new leader would mean other countries — including the United States — would have to defer to China on matters such as peace, trade, and human rights.

That is certainly not a day I want to see anytime soon. To give us our best shot at maintaining — and extending — our position, we must increase our growth in GDP. Clifton concludes that we must maintain a 4.5% growth rate in for sustainable job creation. Even with that, it will take additional work — a GDP growth rate of 5% — to retain leadership of the free world.

Are we currently positioning ourselves to do that?

Winning the future

Western Minnesotans are known as an independent and self-reliant people. The 7th Congressional District which contains 38 of Minnesota's 87 counties range from the Canadian border and follows the western borders with North and South Dakota almost all the way down to Iowa. It was reported by 1890 that more than half of all "Norwegians" in Minnesota lived in the western counties and that many were conservative with a strong moral code. These people are producers and proud of being self-sufficient. They are happy to work, build and create, and need only for the government to leave them to do that.

President Obama's policies are designed to penalize the rich for being rich. The outcome of his policies are however even more sinister as the likely effect will be for the poor to become poorer. America used to be the most accommodating and encouraging nation for people to advance from one economic group to another. The long-lasting effect of the Obama presidency, if his economic principles are allowed to remain, will be an increase in the permanent number of people "captured" by the poor sector. To this date, the 7th Congressional District is a plus 5% Republican district and remains as one of the most conservative districts in Minnesota. Even many of those who historically have voted for the Democratic Party remain conservative and independent-minded. To them, it is a travesty that what used to be grandpa's Democratic Party for the working man, now has become Obama's party for the elite, Hollywood stars who feel guilty for their success and hence promote flawed economic and social agendas, and leftish radicals who seem more driven to change the world for the sake of change than to do good.

To win the future for America, we must work to restore both of our major political parties to realign with the Center principles that formed America's framework of limited federal government, individual responsibility, and free enterprise. These principles do not belong to the Republican Party or the Democratic Party; they belong to the American people. This will require the parent generation to get involved again and lead by example. I have no doubt that a new generation of America's youth again will embrace the American way of self-reliance and drive to pursue opportunities once we lead them to the journey of discovery.

CHAPTER 12

Taxation Strangles Development, Job Creation, Innovation

President Jimmy Carter in 1976 called for a "complete overhaul of our income tax system" and referred to our tax code as "a disgrace to the human race." Since then, the actual U.S. tax code has actually tripled. Go figure! Well, since then, the main reason we have not had a real reform is that complexity is used by politicians and government as a method to hide the true cost of government from the hard-working taxpayers. A true reform and simplification will make the tax burden "visible" and increase "solidarity" among the people. The political and election process demonstrates time after time that it is more concerned about splitting the tax-payers to maintain power.

Erroneous tax policies

Divide and conquer is the most common approach. The demand to tax the rich is the ongoing mantra of envy from the left. The problem we face in America is however not a shortage of tax revenue or that the tax burden is not heavy enough, but rather the excessive size of the federal govern-ment itself. Taxing the rich is nevertheless played out by Obama as a "fairness" issue to gain voters to the detriment of others or more correctly, to the detriment of all. We col-lect more income taxes from the top 1% of earners compared to the bottom 95% percent,[27] a clear example of a divide-and-conquer approach that attempts to pit one set of earners against another.

How long will we tolerate this?

The Cato Institute explains that high earners such as physicians or executives often have unique talents and skills that are factors in their ability to earn more. But penalizing someone with unique skills and talents by requiring him to pay more in taxes could ultimately result in a loss if that per-son chooses to work less because of high taxes. Who would

---

[27] Epstein, Richard. (2011). Design for Liberty. Cambridge: Harvard University Press.

lose? Consumers would lose, as well as our communities who could benefit from the contributions those high earners make. It is absurd to believe that increasing tax rates will increase economic value. An increase in $1 million tax will cost the economy much more than $1 million because of the losses in efficiency caused by taxpayers responding to the higher tax rates. The Congressional Budget Office estimates that each dollar of tax revenue raised costs us from 20 cents to 60 cents more, so we actually lose money when we increase taxes because of the deadweight losses, which are the costs associated with disturbances to — and distractions from — productive activity.[28]

Whichever way we take this fairness game, the reality is that the "fairness" game is a horrific distraction. It prevents us from conducting a serious national discussion on how to prioritize what is affordable or not, what is worthwhile or not, and how to implement a more efficient and transparent system. The fairness game as such remains a clever, yet dishonest method to lure voters to support a position based on an ideological perspective, and is not in the best interest of America since tax rate increases actually kill economic growth and subsequently triggers reductions in tax revenues.

A few national leaders have showed true leadership and championed methods to increase overall tax revenue. And they did so by cutting tax rates in order to grow the economy and the tax base itself. As we review history, we find Presidents John F. Kennedy, Ronald Reagan, Bill Clinton and George W. Bush all in good company by being tax cutters and job creators.

To illustrate that the federal budget cannot be balanced through tax rate increases, I grouped for illustration purposes all the federal tax payers into five groups. Each of the groups contained 20% of all the U.S. tax-filers/returns. I then split the top 20% into three subgroups and titled them the

---

[28] Statement of Chris Edwards, director of tax policy studies at the Cato Institute, before the House Committee on Oversight and Government Reform, February 16, 2011.

Richest 1%, the Rich 7%, and the 12% Well-Off. The other four groups of 20% became the Middle to Upper, Middle, Low to Middle and the Bottom 20%. The exercise then continued by studying various federal budget proposals, including President Obama's 2012 budget plan, President Obama's revised 2013 budget plan (and moving forward), a plan proposal submitted by Paul Ryan (The 2012 Path to Prosperity), and a plan provided by Senators Rand Paul, Mike Lee, and Jim DeMint titled "A Platform to Revitalize America," also referred to as the Tea Party plan. After inserting the various budget proposals into a basic economic model, the model computed how many of the tax-filers (filed tax returns) would see a DOUBLING in total federal taxes in order to balance the federal budget. Without debating the pros and cons of the various budget proposals, the model computed the following:

1) The Paul Ryan Budget (The 2012 Path to Prosperity) required a tax doubling on 9% of all tax-filers.

2) The 3 Senators' Budget (A Platform to Revitalize America) required a doubling of 2.5% of all tax-filers.

3) The two Obama budgets required a doubling in total tax on about 20% of all tax-filers, representing about 38% of all taxpayers (husband and wives).

The conclusion is simple: Without true leadership to explain to the public which programs should be considered for elimination or serious cutbacks and without a commitment to champion intelligent ways to eliminate waste and fraud, it will remain impossible to balance the federal budget. Any attempts to balance the budget through tax rate increases must be viewed only as intentional strategies crafted to postpone decisions that are screaming for solutions: "fix me now!"

Some say, well, we should be bipartisan and compromise to combine tax rate increases with spending cuts to begin the process of reigning in the budget deficits. While being "amenable" sounds good, it is a continued disaster in the making. Yes, the correct answers should go beyond partisanship and focus on economic principles that will do good and no harm. This is achieved if we pursue policies to grow the economic base and overall tax revenue.

Why punish achievement?

During my 2010 U.S. Congressional Campaign, I had the privilege to debate U.S. Representative Collin Peterson on Minnesota Public Radio. The debate took place in Moorhead. One question related to the fairness of increasing taxes on the rich. Peterson answered in line with the traditional Democratic approach to increase taxes on those who can afford more. I turned the question around and asked: "When did it become a sin in America to be successful? Did we not feel a strong sense of pride when we knew someone who achieved success? Secondly, why do we conclude that increasing taxes on the most efficient dollars (from those who create the most jobs) will increase overall tax revenue in the long run?"

Sensible tax policies

How would it work if a government agent is placed at Joe's local retail store to teach them how to increase company revenue by increasing the price of their products? Of course, as any good retailer will tell you, the people at Joe's retail store will reject the agent's suggestion knowing that a price increase will do the opposite and reduce revenue. Increases to product prices beyond the point the marketplace will bear will reduce overall product demand or move demand to other outlets and a corresponding revenue drop. Demand and supply is tied to price and as such is an economic principle which is also applicable to taxation policy. Intelligent tax policy based on proven economic principles demonstrates that a reduction in tax rates motivates and drives producers to expand economic activity and increased job growth for the benefit of all people.

The taxpayers in America are overtaxed and denied prosperity by its wasteful federal government. For those who care to investigate, you will find endless numbers of reports showing waste and fraud. Even the government's own Federal Office of Management and Budget has reported on more than

200 federal programs in which 50% of every tax dollar has been lost to waste and fraud.[29] In terms of taxation, the Heritage Foundation reports that in 2008, the top 1% of earners paid 38% of all federal income taxes, while the bottom 50 percent paid only 3% and 49% of households paid no federal income tax.[30]

When a large percentage of the population pays no federal income tax, we should not be surprised that we have created a fiscal nightmare.

But it's not just personal income taxes that cause problems. At nearly 40%, the U.S. has also the highest corporate income tax rate in the industrialized world, when combining the federal rate with the average rate from the state level, according to the Heritage Foundation. The land of the free has thus become the costliest and least competitive of the developed countries to do business in.

The hard working people of America ought to be outraged not only from the excessive burden that is placed over their shoulders, but that much of this taxation is placed in wasteful programs.

Tax consideration

Until we achieve a tax reform to simplify the tax code, reduce the tax rates, and/or implement some form of a flat or "fair" tax, it is critical to make permanent the Bush-era tax cuts. This is essential to bring certainty for businesses, investors, entrepreneurs, families, working people, and job seekers.

We should lower the corporate income tax to reach equilibrium in tax rates with the average of other industrialized nations. This will eliminate the incentive to move jobs overseas.

Convert capital purchases as immediate expensing to en-

[29] Gruenhagen, Glenn. (2012). Health care in crisis: Is government the solution or the problem? St. Paul: Alethos Press.

[30] Heritage Foundation Blog. Retrieved from http://blog.heritage.org/2012/01/29/chart-of-the-week-top-1-percent-paid-38-percent-of-taxes

courage investments, increase competitiveness, and enhance job creation.

The majority of new jobs are created by small business. Do not penalize small business owners through a higher effective-individual-pass through- tax rate in comparison to the tax rate paid by larger corporations.

Small business produces about half of the private GDP in this country. And we penalize these job creators with a tax compliance cost that is 67% higher than it is for large companies. This compliance costs both in manpower and dollars: It requires 2 billion hours of work and costs the small business sector nearly $19 billion.[31] If we are serious about job creation, then tax simplification is a must.

Stop taxing success as we currently tax successful companies more compared to allowing lower tax rates for inefficient/ ineffective/and/or less profitable companies. For America to remain free and competitive in the world, we should not penalize success and subsidize underperformance.

Permanently eliminate the death tax to help spur the economy, reduce unemployment, and allow for transfer of productive assets from one generation to another. This is vital for the future success of our district in Minnesota to ensure viable transfers of productive assets from generation to generation in order to maintain our base in small-manufacturing, farming, and business in general. The death tax raises only about 1% of the federal tax revenue. But we don't gain much from it because for every $1 raised, roughly $1 is lost in costs related to avoidance, compliance, and enforcement.[32]

This chapter started with using a model to show that the government would need to double the federal tax on 38% of the taxpayers to balance the U.S. yearly budget deficits. Such a tax increase is of course highly irresponsible and detrimental to overall tax revenue. The yearly federal budget deficit was about $160 billion in 2007, $460 billion in 2008,

---

[31] NFIB, Small business growth agenda for the 112th Congress, page 12.

[32] Cato handbook for policy makers, 7th edition. Cato Institute.

and has since escalated to over a trillion per year. The positive impact of growing the economy in terms of increasing or maintaining tax revenues is just as impactful as catching new wind in the sail to power a vessel or nation forward. A simple calculation through the same economic model computes that more than $400 billion can be raised as additional tax revenue, and so without increasing tax rates, if an expanding economy is able to move 15% of the taxpayers from each of the five groups up one level to the next income group, we can see the potential.

Example: If 15% of current no-tax payers are moved into the bottom 20% of taxpayers and 15% of the Middle to Upper are moved into the top 20% of taxpayers etc., we should have no doubt that the combination of sound tax policies, a war on unwarranted and stifling regulations, and a rededication to America's principles of free-enterprise and limited federal government, will set America back on course toward freedom and prosperity. Such combination will not only allow America to again balance its yearly budgets, but ensure that America remains the leader of the free world. A smart tax reform to simplify the tax structure, increase transparency, reduce the overall tax burden, and to grow the economy will again turn America into a magnet for global investments and economic prosperity.

Government does not create long-term sustainable jobs

President Obama's economic plan can only fail because it is not build on sound economic principles. Deficit spending will only speed up and add to the severity of the coming crash we are embarking on. This crash will become unavoidable unless we change direction to take on the challenge from our huge entitlement costs and unleash the free market to reach a GDP growth rate of around 5%. A growth rate close to 5% must be attained for America to remain economically strong and is more than double the current growth rate and future growth rate forecasts based on current policies. Obama and his advisors fall short both in understanding and experience with the power of free enterprise system. They have swallowed hook, line, and sinker the false premises that government can pick winners, buy long-term sustainable jobs, and create real economic growth. They also misunderstood the relationship between innovation and entrepreneurship.

Government can direct investment to speed up innovation in given industries, but it cannot create long-term demand. It is the marketplace which must rule and determine if the ideas, research, and innovation have justifiable value for consumers. The marketplace is at such also a more efficient allocator of capital to access risk and reward compared to government. What eventually will determine if a new product has value in the marketplace is not triggered by government credit lines, stimulus, mandates, or innovation itself. But rather if the new idea or product has the power by itself to unleash a new desire to inspire potential consumers to acquire the new product while willingly forgoing something else of value for its acquisition (time or money). This speaks to the state of mind of more freedom. And this goes back to America's competitive advantage. A people driven to succeed. We are a people with fire in our eyes to innovate, with steel in our will to produce and overcome obstacles, and with love for freedom in the marketplace to select or reject products and ideas. America has greater freedom than China or other nations and therefore should continue to maintain a real competitive advantage if the people are ready to recommit to the American principles of limited government and free enterprise.

CHAPTER 13

Local Communities
Will Restore America

A few years ago, in 2005, two of the companies associated with the parent company of Life-Science Innovations in Willmar faced tremendous difficulties in hiring and moving to Willmar, Minnesota technically advanced people. We would interview, dine, and show various candidates the local community and the benefits of living in Greater Minnesota or as State Senator Bill Ingebrigtsen says: "Better Minnesota." Our two engineering and bio-science companies had the challenge of rapid growth and could not hire fast enough experienced people with advanced technical degrees and experiences. We brought candidates to Willmar, and they would say: "We like the community, the company, the free-flowing lifestyle, and the hardiness of the people in Western-rural Minnesota. We would love to move our families to your community and be part of your companies, but what if we moved and if it did not work out to work for you, who else could we work for that also needed high technical skills with advanced degrees?"

Local leaders can change America

So in the middle of this growth, we began the process of checking other communities that would be "better" suitable for our technical companies. The main criteria involved looking for business communities who could offer broader and deeper opportunities for potential employees, thus making it easier to hire the skills and experiences which our companies needed.

Around this time period of 2005, the State of Minnesota decided to close the State Mental Health Hospital in Willmar. This site included about 30 buildings, 400,000 square feet of potential office space, and 100 beautiful acres, all located in close view of Willmar Lake. The site looked like a college campus, but as the number of patients had reduced from 1,200 to a few hundred individuals, the size of the campus and the associated administrative cost had become unsustainable for the State of Minnesota. The site was now a big, white, elephant for the state, which desperately was looking for a buyer with redevelopment plans that would be good for the community. The leadership of our affiliated companies decided to visit the hospital site for various considerations, but I don't think any of us seriously believed we could make the hospital site pencil out for the purpose of our two technology companies.

The CEO of Life-Science Innovations is Ted Huisinga, and he is one-of-a-kind. I am privileged to have worked for him and been mentored by him for about 18 years. Ted was 82 when the rest of this story transpired. He is now 87 and still works every day from about 9 am to 5/6 p.m. or for as long as there is action in the office. Ted's favorite saying when describing himself is: "I live in tomorrow."

He grew up in the local Dutch-Christian-Reformed Community, pursued education in music at the University of Minnesota, joined the Army and served in Japan. When he completed his service, Ted came back to the community and began to work for his uncle and soon took over the management of Willmar Poultry Company. Over the next 60 years, Ted and his team grew the company and the turkey industry in Minnesota together with Earl B. Olson, the founder of Jennie-O Turkey Company, and many growers from the community. Today, the Minnesota turkey industry directly employs about 7,000 and about 8,000 in spin-off industries, according to the Minnesota Turkey Growers Association. Minnesota remains the number one turkey state in the country, exporting about 90 percent of the Minnesota turkey productions out of state. Four of the top five most producing turkey counties in Minnesota reside within the 7th Congressional District in Minnesota and include Kandiyohi, Stearns, Becker, and Otter Tail.

Throughout the years, Ted and his partner Ray Norling reinvested the earnings from the company into further growth within the turkey industry, but also used their entrepreneurial drive and love for innovation to expand into engineering and bioscience. The initial focus was always to use innovation as a method to add more value to the core business in the turkey industry, but many discoveries and successes came from a combination of hard work, intentional planning, and coincidences. This combination turned discoveries into new business ventures and contain the potential to exceed the historical core businesses.

During a corporate board meeting scheduled to review the various potential locations as relocation sites for the research divisions of the technical companies, the young leadership team was asked to present the pros and cons of the various sites, highlighting some very attractive tax incentives offered by certain communities in order to encourage a selection of their locations. By then the potential to purchase the State Hospital in Willmar had become a scenario, but it was far fledged, and not considered a competitive option in terms of net present values. As the discussion moved forward in consideration of moving, Ted finally said: "Well, boys, you can move anywhere you want." And then he chuckled, paused, and said: "As long your move is within the boundaries of our County (Kandiyohi)!"

The rest of us looked at each other thinking: Ted, are you seriously thinking of the big, white, elephant? The hospital which the state is looking for a buyer?

So we challenged Ted: "You have taught us all these years to watch the bottom line, to be conservative, while also looking beyond the horizon for something great to will into being! But this option is risky. If it fails, it can take us under."

We needed to know more. "Ted, what is this about?" We asked humorously. "Is this about your 'ego'?"

Ted smiled and said: "No, this is about self-satisfaction."

He went on to explain. "This is about leading, knowing that you will be part of something bigger than yourself. This is about doing something for the next generation."

By now, the size of Ted's vision was hanging over us, but we could see "fire" in his eyes as he laid out his vision of what this could become. "Imagine the largest, private, business, enterprise, discovery center in the nation."

He wanted us to imagine what the site could become for the community and greater Minnesota as we would have something attractive to encourage the next generation of youth from the community to return to after they completed their advanced degrees, acquired some real work experiences, and grew tired of the big-city life.

Well, we thought, *if Ted is willing to embrace such a grand adventure to create a business and technology campus at this point in his career, then we should join him to make the vision come true.* Over the next 10 months, we entered a grueling period of complex negotiations with the State of Minnesota, Kandiyohi County, the City of Willmar, the local Economic Development Corporation, and union representatives. It was like shadow boxing. As soon as there was agreement between two groups, others would stand up in disagreement.

We went through several points along the way when we believed the deal was dead.

In one meeting which included representatives from each group, the discussion was so unproductive and heated that the group at large concluded the negotiations were over and could not be settled. As all stood up to leave the room, I asked: "When the news media calls, what message will we provide to explain that a deal could not be reached? Can we identify the top three reasons for a severed deal?"

There was no response to my questions and one by one the various leaders went back to the negotiation table. After a few minutes of discussion, we reached agreements on the various points between the state, county, city, union and us representing the buyer and free enterprise. MinnWest Technology Campus in Willmar was thus born.

The technology campus in Willmar, 7 years later, today serves as the site for 350 private jobs covering various roles in business from leadership to management to administration. It serves several industries including engineering, bioscience, consulting, child care, and restaurants.

Over 30 different private companies are locating on campus representing industries from genetics, nutrition, agriculture, design and manufacturing of automation equipment, production of vaccines for food safety, services, etc. The private ownership of the campus has invested over $14 million dollars so far into the development of the campus. The most recent development includes the formation of a joint project with the University of Minnesota to create the Mid-Central Research and Outreach Center. The private owners donated a fully restored building to the university to match a DEED grant of $1.25 million. The university will provide the faculty and run the center. The goal for this center includes uniting private companies with university faculty and students to advance technology and job creation within the State and Greater Minnesota.

The process of rebuilding the economic strength of America will only succeed if it is led by local leaders in each community.

It is with confidence I can highlight that much innovation and entrepreneurship is taking place in the midst of people in smaller communities.

It is always interesting to read the expressions of visitors. This is especially true when offering tours to visitors from larger companies and the international community. As they visit our operation in Willmar, Minnesota, it is not uncommon to hear something along these lines: "Well, I never imagined this much innovation and business drive would grow in the middle of a 'corn field'." For those of us who live in Greater Minnesota (or the Better Minnesota), we are not surprised because we know that, where we live, this is the place where all the children are above average anyway.

Local growth reduces our dependence on the federal government

Local leaders who are committed to this country understand that rebuilding the economic strength of America rests with them. When our local communities grow, our schools grow. Schools are the lifeblood of many small communities. As our schools go, so go our communities. Bringing jobs to communities is not just about what happens in those individual businesses, it is also about creating opportunities that affect the entire area.

Bringing jobs affects wealth creation for residents. That allows residents to give back to charities and their churches. Those charities and churches serve people in need. All of a sudden all of those efforts — local job creation, local school improvements, local church and charity giving — are minimizing the dependence on the government because the community is able to do more.

Local leaders, especially business owners and entrepreneurs, who understand this realize it's not just about them. It's about serving humanity and their communities. And that creates more value than government ever can.

Residents breathe life into communities through commitment

Randy Nordin of Podco shares his company's story.

Nordin grew up in a family of 12 on a little farm east of Lancaster, in Kittson County. "We've always been community-minded and worked really hard to keep this small town and county going. It's a county that used to have 10,000 and is under 5,000 now."

Nordin said he's been involved in many meetings and discussions about ways to help the area. "Podco itself was generated out of a meeting with corporations and vice presidents and bankers... At the end of the meeting, I asked the corporate vice president and the bankers, 'What is it that us folks over here in Kittson County can do that you don't like to do?'"

They had seen declines in industry and employment. He mentioned one company that went from employing about 800 in the Lancaster area to about 100. "We got real scared. We wanted our school to keep going."

Nordin was looking for ideas. He knew the area needed something by way of new employment. Those discussions and ideas ultimately resulted in Podco, a company he formed with his siblings in 2002.

Podco produces a high-quality finish process for manufactured parts. "Four of us brothers and one sister decided to talk to banks because we didn't have much cash."

He met with bankers and shared his idea. "Our family is widely known for integrity," Nordin said. "In that meeting, they promised me $150,000 without knowing anything about our finances."

Podco would be a way the Nordin family could help the small community. It wasn't easy. "The first year, we had sales of $14,000 and one employee," Nordin said. "We just about walked away from it several times."

But they hung in there, because they knew it wasn't just about them. It was about Lancaster. "We were profitable around year seven or eight," he said. Today, the company employs 25 people.

"We took the concept that 'I don't care if I walk away without a penny' because we really wanted to do something for the community. We were tired of seeing young people walking away."

Nordin has had a lifelong commitment to that community. When he was younger, he moved to Minneapolis and played ball. "The district superintendent came the last three days with $10,000 in his briefcase to try to convince me to stay. But my wife and I took it upon ourselves that we were going to raise our family in a rural setting, no matter what money we turned down."

So they did.

That commitment continued over the years and remains strong with the decision ten years ago to establish Podco in Lancaster. He doesn't see it as a disadvantage or feel that he gave up something by choosing the town. "We could not have done it cheaper somewhere else. Our land is cheaper, construction is cheaper. Most families can work at a little less wage so we have that advantage over any metro area around."

Podco produces environmentally friendly finishes for a variety of surfaces, including aluminum, iron, glass, ceramic, and plastic. A dye sublimation patent means future growth potential.

"It's been very good, impact on community. For example, in this town of 365, the annual payroll is over half a million dollars, from this one business. We have other small businesses where we bring them work and they bring us work."

Nordin and his wife raised four children of their own and a nephew and is happy his children have decided to stay around the area. "The good Lord has been good to us. We have all four of our children here with us and 12 grandchildren. One is a teacher. One is a registered nurse. One son has a construction management degree and had big offers in Florida and Texas and turned them down to come back here."

Another son moved back and bought the local lumber yard.

"It makes me feel very good that this concept is working. There were times that my wife would say that she was beginning to wonder about my sanity. When you have a son who is working there and the business is failing … ." Nordin said, recalling the early years before the company started turning a profit. "For three or four years I couldn't sleep a wink."

But the commitment, work, and sacrifice are paying off now. "Hard work is really where it's at. We've noticed no recession in this area. We were nervous about that. We have corporate clients all over the world. People around here are willing to do anything to be employed. That's the key. Keeps a recession away."

It will take people like Nordin, who are committed to their local communities and aren't afraid to put in the hard work to look for solutions. He could have given up on his town. He could have gone elsewhere. But he didn't. He loves the heartland, and it shows.

That is the love that will turn around this country.

Servant leadership makes difference
to communities, large and small

Dan Malmstrom grew up in central Minnesota. He came from a very middle class family. Neither of his parents was college-educated, but they had an incredible work ethic. "They taught all their kids to work hard," Malmstrom said. "We had jobs and started our own businesses when we were in the eighth grade. We were told that they were probably not going to have any money to send us to college."

So he started his own lawn mowing business in the eighth grade. He graduated from his high school as valedictorian and with a scholarship. He picked a college — Concordia College in Moorhead — without ever having stepped on a college campus. "You play baseball and you look at people and see people with a good, Christian ethics. I played with a guy, Dave Freeman. He took me under his wing. Dave chose Concordia College. That was the only thing to gauge what college was. I thought, if Concordia is good enough for Dave, it's good enough for me."

In his junior year, he went to the placement director. "I'm going to be a senior next year, and I've worked my way through. I need to have an internship. The second day of class my senior year came up to me. She said, 'Dan, Dan, I've got an internship opportunity for you.'"

She instructed him to wear a suit, tie, and dress shoes for the interview. "I said, 'I don't have a suit. I don't have a tie, and I don't have any dress shoes,'" Malmstrom said. He didn't have money for extras. "I was eating venison, which I shot on the weekend and canned vegetables from my mother's garden."

The interview was with IBM. He made it to the interview, but turned down the job because he didn't think he wanted to work in sales. "They must have liked me or something and couldn't believe I turned it down."

So he reconsidered and decided to take the internship. He worked 20 or 30 hours a week while in school and went to work for IBM full-time after graduation. "I went to school with IBM after I graduated. I learned software engineering, languages, database."

He graduated from IBM's technical institute as a top performer. "I will become IBM's national rookie of the year," he told his supervisor.

The supervisor thought Malmstrom was a bit naïve. He suggested Malmstrom strive for something a little less ambitious, such as regional rookie of the year. Malmstrom, though, kept his goal. "Fourteen months later, I was standing on stage for two solid weeks at every IBM 100% club. I stood on the stage with the president of IBM as IBM's national rookie of the year."

He continued to do well and in 1987 one of his small customers in Fargo, North Dakota, Great Plains Software invited him to leave IBM and work there. "The president of Great Plains Software ... had the Midwest work ethic just like me. His family bought this little company called Great Plains. They were my customers at IBM, but they never bought anything from me. This guy had this vision of creating this software company on the plains of North Dakota. He convinced me I needed to leave IBM and go work for Great Plains."

He prayed about it and decided to leave. An IBM vice president flew in to try to convince him to change his mind. "He looks at me and says this software company you are talking about, I guarantee that company will not exist in ten years."

Ten years later, in June 1997, Great Plains had a successful initial public offering and a couple of years later sold to Microsoft for $1.1 billion.

He recalls that ten-year span. "We were kids who were smart, with meager beginnings, who worked hard and created our own destiny."

That Midwest work ethic helped them hang in there. "There were many times we didn't have money to make payroll," he said, remembering being turned down for bank loans. "We bootstrapped it until the point of the public offering and that sale to Microsoft."

Malmstrom said Great Plains spurred lots of other business in the area. "You can count more than 50 software companies in Fargo today. At the time, we were the only one. There is that Midwest ethic. I didn't need a handout. I don't need government regulation to get in the way. What I need is entrepreneurial spirit. Freedom and liberty to go and do the American Dream. If you have the work ethic, the rest will fall into place. That was just the beginning of my experience."

Since that time, he has started six companies. He was one of the founding executives for Great Plains, taking it from one product line to multiple product lines and from one country to 150 countries. "It wasn't about me. It was about us. The vision of what we could build. We wanted to build a company that Microsoft would want."

Malmstrom, now in Alexandria, Minnesota as president of Douglas Scientific, points to servant leadership as an important element. It hearkens back to Judeo-Christian principles. "Alexandria has an executive Christian ethic that is unbelievable. I've traveled around the world, and I've never seen anything like this in my life. From CEO to CEO these guys are servant leaders and these guys have turned their businesses over to God. There is something here that is nowhere else in the world. These guys help each other. They want each other to succeed. They give back their profits to the kingdom work."

Douglas Scientific launched as a division of Douglas Machine in 2009 before becoming incorporated the following year. It has gone from three employees to about 80. "We built a great company. The culture here is amazing. We have a mission. Our mission is what drives us every day. Our mission is that we will make the world a better place by delivering innovative laboratory automation."

Malmstrom's servant leadership style plays out in everything he does. He hired a new employee who needed an office, so he gave his up to the new employee.

"Here is where that stems from: It's part of our culture that is really important. We hire this way. There is no one more important than the mission... Everyone on my entire team and in my company understands that the most important thing we have is a sensitivity and understanding of how every one of us connects to the mission. Me not having an office is just one example of many where the employees know the mission is more important than me. Somehow we are losing that in America."

Faith community is key to health of local areas

A group of seven Willmar business leaders met in 2006 to discuss our responsibilities as business leaders beyond the expectation of creating profits and jobs. Profits and jobs are both important to the health of a community, of course. But we also realized there was more to building a thriving place to call home.

This group of seven leaders focused on how to help co-workers and employees to better cope through life's many challenges. The focus of the group thereafter expanded itself to making a real difference in our local community. The group formalized as Willmar Area Faith @Work as a non-profit with the simple goal of bringing unity through Christ to the Willmar area. From the start, Faith @ Work sought to equip members of the marketplace by providing prayer support, programs, and encouragement centered on a solid Christian foundation. Some specific programs which arose from these efforts are:

• Community Prayer: held every week for the public to address challenges in the community

• Business Connections: a time for business leaders to share, discuss, and pray

• Leadership Development: courses to train leaders to enhance their reach and effectiveness through servant leadership

• Chaplaincy Program: proactive and personalized employee assistance program. Companies have assigned male, female, and ethnically diverse chaplains who visit worksites regularly, and are available for crisis care, any needed help, and confidential discussions.

Willmar Area Faith @ Work also organized special projects for the community at large, but has been careful about not intruding on community efforts which already may be underway by other organizations. These special projects are vetted by testing if the outcome will have enduring value to the recipient.

Examples:

1) Organized members from nine Willmar churches along with local emergency and law enforcement personnel for a joint worship service on the tenth anniversary of the September 11th attack. The donation from the event of about $38,000 was used to purchase two emergency rescue vehicles for the community.

2) Carried out event with more than 1,200 volunteers from 29 Willmar area churches to package 306,000 meals to be sent to Somali refugee camps in east Africa. More than $43,000 was raised to ship these meals to refugee camps.

3) Work with local pastors to develop a program aimed at restoring fatherhood in our local community. This will involve an event to focus on fatherlessness, but such event must become an on-going process to ensure continuity. The program will challenge fathers who already are doing well with their own children to step up by also helping kids without active fathers, as well as helping fathers who can and should do better with their own kids. The program will also help to restore those men who are disconnected from their children. The discussion among these pastors and leaders highlighted the importance of ongoing mentoring and a process for accountability between pastors and the men in the various churches who elect to stand in the gap as fathers for others.

What Randy Nordin is doing at PODCO, Dan Malmstrom is doing at Douglas Scientific, and what business leaders are doing through Willmar Area Faith @ Work are all examples of ways locals can make an impact in their communities to help rebuild America.

These are by no means isolated instances. People are

doing similar things in communities across Minnesota and across this country. We need more to join.

CHAPTER 14

It Is All Connected
(why we can't focus
on just one issue)

W e've spent an entire book outlining the problems that face America and what needs to be done about them. Many people will agree on the problems, but may not choose to do anything about them. It's not that they are bad people. They just see the solution as somebody else's job, after all, they are busy working, running businesses, raising children, running organizations, and doing the other pursuits of daily life.

They can compartmentalize their lives and see no need to become a part of the solution, though they can readily identify the problems.

Unfortunately, compartmentalization won't work here.

It's tempting to think America's problems affect only one area of life or can be solved by one group of people. It's tempting to think that if we address the family or faith or free enterprise, that we will get back on the right track. It's also tempting to think that if we simply focus on getting rid of big government, that life will be great.

But that is not the case. We can't compartmentalize what's wrong with America, nor can we compartmentalize the solution. We must address all the points we've discussed in this book, and we must discuss them all now. Together.

It used to be that every part of life flowed into the other. Our faith was a part of our work and our work was a part of our family life. We had entire families who lived and worked together on farms and in family businesses.

Today, everything is separate and in its own compartment. Our work lives are separate from our home lives. Our faith lives are separate from our careers. Who we are at home is different from who we are outside. We go to work and never mention our faith, whether for fear of governmental regulations that tell us we can't do so because of the risk of offending someone else or because we don't want to be judged.

And when it comes to fixing what's wrong with America, we try to compartmentalize even that. We try to separate the social changes from economics. We try to separate government regulations from taxation.

But those are all false separations. That is because each

piece affects the other. Our faith affects our work. Social changes have economic impacts. Who we are at home affects who we are at work.

Perhaps the most devastating part of all this compartmentalization is the thing most people don't even realize they've compartmentalized God. We have de-emphasized God in America by relegating Him to an afterthought. We have relegated Him to a small portion of our lives, rather than integrating Him into every segment. We removed the big "G" (God in whom we trust) from our schools and replaced Him with small "g"— government. We used to see God as the Ultimate factor in our decision-making. Now He is merely one consideration, if that.

The Modern Compartmentalized Life

WE REDEFINED GOD FROM BEING THE CIRCLE AND MOVED HIM INSIDE THE CIRCLE TO A LIMITED ROLE

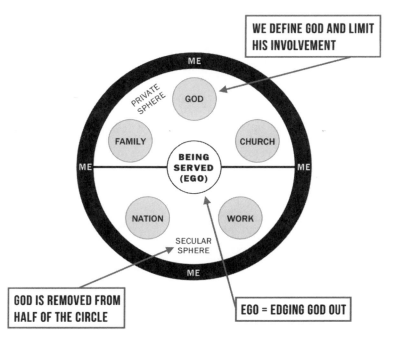

WE DEFINE GOD AND LIMIT HIS INVOLVEMENT

ME

PRIVATE SPHERE

GOD

FAMILY

CHURCH

ME

BEING SERVED (EGO)

ME

NATION

WORK

SECULAR SPHERE

ME

GOD IS REMOVED FROM HALF OF THE CIRCLE

EGO = EDGING GOD OUT

The illustration on the previous page shows just how we have shoved God to the side and made Him equal to other factors in our lives.

We no longer consider that He is the Creator who has given us not only our lives but this country. Instead, we pull Him out only as needed or as is convenient, and tuck Him safely away at all other times.

That is the reason we have been able to make such decisions as legalizing abortion. For if God were still as important in American life as He once was, such a decision would never have even been considered.

Deemphasizing God also has led to a weakening of our moral character and willingness to be of service to others. We are in love with self, often to the exclusion of participation in anything that does not directly benefit us. We no longer engage in pursuits for the greater good.

Instead, we compartmentalize service, often leaving it for others. We decide, after all, that it's somebody else's job to teach our children, build up our communities, and serve our neighbors.

If we are to build a real and sustainable movement to rebuild America, we cannot continue to live compartmentalized lives. We must unite all of our interests into one common purpose, that of getting our country back on track.

CHAPTER 15

What This All Means to You

Dan Malmstrom's point about servant leadership is one we can all take to heart. Servant leadership is when we give priority and attention to those we serve. We contribute to the well-being of the world around us. We can all be servant leaders in this movement. Movement requires sacrifice

That is where the approach of servant leadership comes in. This movement will require individuals to look to serve others and to be leaders who help their country through a difficult patch.

Any time you go against what is commonly thought or done, you will meet resistance. And a movement like this will not only have resistance, but it will require short-term sacrifice from those who choose to become involved. What are those sacrifices? We must sacrifice time, resources, even some personal desires. All for the common good of our fellow man and our country. All for our children's futures.

Sacrificing time may mean putting in hours to attend events to properly educate others about the dangers we face, rather than spending time on a favored recreational activity. Sacrificing resources may mean allocating your talents, money, or other assets to the movement, even when you could use those assets for other means. Sacrificing personal desires may mean putting off a "fun" vacation for a while so you can dedicate your time to making sure this movement succeeds.

These sacrifices won't be easy, but know that they are part of allowing the self — you — to serve the greater good — the future of our nation.

Sacrifice isn't called for only by a few of us, but by all of us. Even me. Calling for this movement wasn't an easy decision on my part, and it hasn't gone without my own sacrifices. I am in the middle of a very successful career in business. I get to work with people whose opinions matter. In fact, I work for a man who has been a mentor and friend to me for more than 18 years. We're doing good work and truly making an impact in Willmar and well beyond.

But as I looked around this country that I love and I saw

the devastation being brought by politicians in Washington, I realized I could no longer continue as I had been. While my contribution to my local community is very important to me, I realized I had to use whatever gifts, talents, time, and resources, God has blessed me with, to do what I could for our country. And so began my work for this movement.

I paused my corporate career to bring together like-minded people who also are concerned about the direction in which our nation is going. This is about lifting up each community at home and taking those communities to Washington. A movement needs to be much bigger than one individual. It has to be much bigger than me. It needs to be focused on what we can do together in a way we haven't done before.

CHAPTER 16

The Final Inning (America's game)

We started the book with an analogy using America's favorite pastime, baseball. You remember the scene: We have two teams facing off, America's We the People Team against the star closer from the Centralized Federal Government Team. The star closer is President Barack Obama. He is ready to transform and finish the game. It is the bottom of the ninth inning. The Centralized Federal Government Team is leading 3-0. The bases are loaded. Can the People's Team come back? The count is 2 outs. One more out and it is over.

America's team has limited government on first base. It is a long way to home plate. A long time has passed since we had a limited federal government for the people. The player on first base can hardly remember how free and strong they used to be when they were allowed to make decisions on their own.

On second base, free enterprise is representing America's Team. The second base player looks a bit better than the first base player. Free enterprise is comprised of small business owners, the entrepreneurs - who take risks and create most of the jobs in our nation. But free enterprise is also comprised of medium to large companies. Many of the larger companies have by now accepted big government and the expensive regulations. They actually have learned to take advantage of the expensive regulations and use them against the smaller companies who cannot carry the burden. Many of the big companies actually give just as much donations to big government political candidates as small government candidates. Nevertheless, free enterprise as a player still remembers the feeling of being free to explore, take chances, fail, succeed, and grow. The free enterprise player is hoping for a grand slam to bring them all home.

On third base, we have America's families. These are the people who work day by day to make a living. Many of them have forgotten how they used to be free and self-sufficient. They are not sure how hard they want to play against the star closer. After all, why worry when the star closer and the Central Government team promised them that all will be fine regardless of the outcome of the game. But when you look a little closer, behind some of the confusion, behind some of the struggling families, there is still fire in the eyes of many people. They are ready to run all the way home. They not only remember freedom and opportunity. They not only hope for a grand slam. They are praying for a grand slam. You can see them seek a Higher Power, as they pray in humility, as they reach out to each other. "God bless our America. We will get back on your side, God. Lord, give us speed and strength to reach home plate. Forgive us for our negligence. Give us another chance, and we will restore our nation. We will bring you back into our families, our schools, and into our government."

The count remains two outs. President Obama needs only one more strike or a chase to end the game. He is the closer. Many star pitchers came before him to give him the lead. All he needs to do is to finish the game. All he needs to do is to transform the nation for good. No going back. As a closer, all he needs to do is to prevent the farmer from hitting the ball out of the park. If he can throw a strike or fool the farmer to chase a ball, he wins regardless.

So here we are. Obama's first strike to the farmer was the continued subsidies from the Centralized Government. The subsidy ball confused the farmer. He knew he was a good producer and that he was freer than anyone else to speak his mind. Then he remembered clearly that the world valued his production. He knew he was needed as a farmer and had much to offer. The world's demand for food and energy would double in the future. His future was bright; he could transition out of those subsidies and remain successful. He swing and missed. Strike one.

The second ball was regulations, EPA, CAP&TRADE. This ball made him just mad. He swung and missed. Strike two.

The farmer is watching the closer. He sees the ball – it is national healthcare. The ball is clear in his sight. He not only dislikes what this ball will do by forcing him for the first time to purchase something from the federal government whether he wants it or not. He knows it is about much more than this ball. He knows this ball will end the game and it will transform his country. This ball will confirm that there is nothing a Centralized Government can't do. As the ball leaves the pitcher's glove, it becomes bigger, clearer, and he sees it in slow motion. This ball can change his life. He knows he will not miss it. He knows he can not miss it. He does not miss it!

It is a grand slam!

And now go and make the rest of the story.

CHAPTER 17

Where We Go From Here

I've laid out the reasoning for this movement. Our nation was founded on ideals we no longer live by but we have gone seriously off course. As a result, we are in danger of becoming an over-taxed, over-regulated country of European leanings and diminishing world influence, led by China.

Our families are in peril, as children grow up where fathers no longer seem relevant. Families and small businesses are becoming increasingly burdened with new taxation, even though it's a verifiable fact that each new tax dollar costs more than it raises.

Business has become stymied as entrepreneurs and small business owners are hesitant to invest in the current economic climate for fear their investment will be wasted due to policy decisions by inexperienced and uninformed bureaucrats.

Certain sectors of the economy, while doing well in the midst of downturns everywhere else, face increasing challenges that could drain them of profitability and viability. One such sector, agriculture, is facing mounting pressure by activists, counterproductive regulations, and resistance to technology.

At the root of every one of these challenges is one thing: Washington, D.C. Washington, D.C. is the common denominator in America's problems. Because of that, America must fix Washington.

Many Washington bureaucrats and policymakers have gotten so disconnected from the heart of this country that they have forgotten the people, are confused about what is best, and uninterested in making real and significant improvements.

But people in the heartland have not forgotten.

We know it is up to us to take back our country, correct course, and save us all. For this generation and those to come.

It is not too late for us.

Come join us. Let's all join as builders of the land. Be a part of the One American Movement.

The One American Movement will restore the ideals that made us great and return to the America our Founding Fathers envisioned. It is up to us.

Join the movement!

CHAPTER 18

The Byberg Campaign Framework

In this time of crisis and opportunity, America doesn't just need a new set of policies. It needs the birth of a new kind of politics.

That's why I am taking a real risk and am running a different kind of campaign. A campaign that's not just about doing whatever is possible to win, but about doing what is right and deserving to win.

Every candidate thinks she deserves to win. Running for office is hard, and takes more than a little ego. But a lot of candidates want to win so much that they forget that deserving to win requires integrity, and the willingness to not just take the risk of being honest with voters about what you believe, but the willingness to listen to voters and become their servant.

Servant leadership works in business, and will work in politics if the politicians would just start listening to the voters and focusing not on what "can be done" in today's hyperpartisan atmosphere, but what needs to be done to rekindle the American Dream.

Politicians who care only about getting elected no longer deserve to be.

A different kind of campaign

When my wife Nancy and I decided to jump into the fray and run for Congress, we made a commitment to running with integrity, principles, advice from our peers, and local support. We believed that we had to be worthy to win.

We call these the cornerstones of our campaign, and developed a formal structure to ensure that these cornerstones truly are the foundation of our campaign.

Advisory & Accountability Board

Integrity in campaigning can only exist if it actually extends into governing. To that end the first thing I did was recruit an advisory & accountability board to keep myself and my team firmly grounded.

Restoring the integrity of our national political process does not begin in Washington; it starts at home with how we conduct ourselves in the midst of "we the people."

How many politicians do you know who have been in office for more than four years who stick to their principles? No one man or woman can do this alone.

Because of this, we recruited men and women of the highest caliber from throughout the district to join the advisory & accountability board. They come from many different perspectives, including private business. Some are experienced political activists.

While they may not always agree on all individual policies, I am leading by seeking to be held accountable to voters, and these leaders, on three governing principles (the three governing principles are defined further below).

Each of the board members has agreed to serve in this capacity, not only up to the election in November of 2012; but also during Congressional term.

In a typical political campaign, people are hired as staff for the life cycle of the campaign. When it is over, these staffers go back to wherever they came from. So networking or relationships tend to be short-lived and severed after the campaign.

My framework of a long-standing advisory-accountability board ensures long-term connectivity between the candidate/representative and the local leaders and between these "board" members and other leaders throughout the district.

Principles

1) Liberty: Derived from Limited Federal Government (resulting in Sensible Local Government).Thomas Jefferson: "Good government is limited government and ... limited government encourages our civic happiness."

2) Pursuit of Happiness: Experienced through Free Enterprise.

Ronald Reagan: "Entrepreneurs and their small enterprises are responsible for almost all the economic growth in the United States."

3) Life: Secured through a Moral Code.

John Adams: "Our Constitution was made only for a moral and religious people. It is wholly inadequate to the government of any other."

•

Each principle is essential to the other.

Liberty without a moral code leads to anarchy! Individual responsibility is derived from having a moral code. A moral code gives us a backbone, without it people cannot be self-governed because they will violate the basic rights of others. Limited Government, therefore, can't exist without a basic moral code. If people are incapable of self-governance due to a lack of such basic moral code, then Free Enterprise cannot succeed in a reality of Limited Government.

It is, however, possible to restore our American economic prosperity and the pursuit of happiness. A new and long lasting dedication by our people, to a moral code, will replace the bureaucratic inefficiencies and cost of big government, with the "speed of trust."

No nation can compete with America or any other nation whose people elect to be wired to basic principles. Such code will restore America as the land of opportunity.

Heritage Alliance

It can be a daunting task to penetrate this large district with the right message. Doing so will take a team of motivated people from throughout the district, which will own up to their responsibilities as American citizens. Our government could not have gained the incredible power they exhibit today if we had not willingly allowed them to take it. This is OUR nation, and OUR elected officials are there to serve us, not the opposite. It's time for us to reassert our ownership in the United States of America.

The Heritage Alliance is a motivated, grassroots group of supporters and activists who will receive regular updates and will be equipped with a clear message of the campaign. These are people who will boldly share our message with family, friends, and neighbors.

But the Heritage Alliance is more. It is also the people we rely upon not just to spread our message, but help shape it.

None of us has all the answers, but together all of us do.

The 400 Club

Money fuels a campaign. A contribution is your exercise of free will. If you can't finance a great message, it most likely will not be heard by enough voters to accomplish victory.

The 400 Club is focused on people who have the capacity to support our campaign with significant contributions. It is made up of community leaders, enterprise leaders, farmers and retirees, who believe in a government of the people ... by the people ... and for the people.

Restoring America is not just about what you say, but also about how you elect to live or even more what you elect to BE.

The 400 Club is the culmination of our vision to deserve to win, by first winning over the people who can help get us over the top. My opponent gets over 80% of his campaigns funds from either special interest groups and/or from outside our state; I aim to get over 80% of my funds from individuals within the 7th District.

The only way to do that is to ask people who have never given before to give, and give a lot, to help us get our message out. We named this group the "400 Club" because we need at least 400 people to give $1,000 or more to our campaign in order to win. And we are well on our way to accomplishing that goal.

We are building our campaign on these cornerstones because we believe that just winning is not enough.

Deserving to win will be the secret to our success not just

this November, but in Washington.

We'd love to have your help.

Contact us at:

Lee Byberg, P.O. Box 429, Willmar, MN 56201

lee@bybergforcongress.com or vlee.byberg@gmail.com

Which One Are You?

Are You a Builder?

I watched them tearing a building down, a gang of men in a busy town.

With a ho-heave-ho and a lusty yell, they swung a beam and a side wall fell.

I asked the foreman, are these men skilled, the kind you'd hire if you had to build?

He gave a laugh and said no indeed, just common labor is all I need.

Why, I can easily wreck in a day or two what builders have taken years to do!

I thought to myself as I went my way, which of these roles have I tried to play.

Am I a builder who works with care, measuring life by rule or square?

Am I shaping my life to a well-made plan, patiently doing the best I can,

Or am I a wrecker who walks the town, content with the labor of tearing down?

— *Author Unknown*

Addendum

Prayer for America by President Thomas Jefferson

Offered a National Prayer for Peace on March 4, 1805:
"Almighty God, Who has given us this good land for our heritage; We humbly beseech Thee that we may always prove ourselves a people mindful of Thy favor and glad to do Thy will. Bless our land with honorable ministry, sound learning, and pure manners. Save us from violence, discord and confusion, from pride and arrogance, and from every evil way. Defend our liberties, and fashion into one united people the multitude brought hither out of many kindreds and tongues. Endow with Thy spirit of wisdom those whom in Thy Name we entrust the authority of government, that there may be justice and peace at home, and that through obedience to Thy law, we may show forth Thy praise among the nations on the earth. In time of prosperity fill our hearts with thankfulness, and in the day of trouble, suffer not our trust in Thee to fail; all of which we ask through Jesus Christ our Lord, Amen." [33]

[33] Federer, William J. America's God and Country, Encyclopedia of Quotations. Pp 327-328.

About the Author

Lee Byberg is currently the Republican-endorsed candidate for Congress in Minnesota's 7th Congressional district.

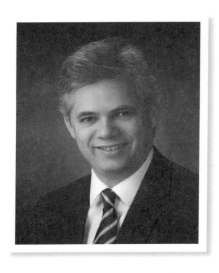

Byberg has a unique background. Born in Chicago, IL in 1962, he was raised by Christian missionary parents in Brazil, Paraguay, and Norway, where he acquired his distinctive Norwegian accent. Lee moved to Minnesota in 1982 after graduating from high school and attended the University of Minnesota, Carlson School of Management, where he obtained his Bachelor of Science in Business Administration (1987), and a Masters of Business Administration (1990).

Lee is currently Vice President of Operations for Life-Science Innovations in Willmar. Lee started his career as an associate with the public accounting firm Coopers and Lybrand. He then worked as a senior economic consultant for Phillips Petroleum Company. After spending three years with Phillips Petroleum, Lee made his way to Willmar, Minnesota and became the director of planning and economics for Willmar Poultry Company. In 2003, Lee became the general manager of Willmar Poultry. After a successful thirteen-year tenure with Willmar Poultry Company, Lee was named vice president of operations for Life-Science Innovations, the parent company of Willmar Poultry.

Lee's background instilled in him an appreciation of and fascination with American government and history. His experience in South America and Norway gives him a unique love of the free enterprise system, and the wisdom of

America's founding fathers. It is this love of America and its free enterprise system that has led Lee to run for Congress.

Lee and his wife Nancy reside in Willmar, MN and have three sons, Kristoffer, Anders, and Steffen. Lee is a member in the Sons of Norway organization, Willmar Area Faith @ Work, and the Willmar Lakes Chamber of Commerce. Lee and Nancy are members of the Willmar Assembly of God Church. Lee is a dedicated family man and enjoys serving in his community.

For Information

Lee Byberg, P.O. Box 429, Willmar, MN 56201
lee@bybergforcongress.com or vlee.byberg@gmail.com